Luncheon/Dinner   Date _____

Menu

...est of Dove
...uckes
...llops—mustard sauce
Little soup
toast
...icken vermouth—mushrooms
Chinese peas
...eekie + leekie salad
corn bread
...all puffs of ice cream
...colate sauce
...la
1963   *Wines*
— Mary Lee

Mary Lee
Slee r
Douglas

Menu

bread of wild dove
tarameek balls
caviar thereos

onion soup
peppernickle toast
chicken vermouth
mushrooms
chinese peas
endive salad + beetle
corn bread
English toffee ice-cream
cake for Jimmie's birthday

Flowers

swans—pink carnations

Gown & Jewels worn   red satin p j—with sk...

Ocl...

Cunahello + File...
Mall + Rac...
Jimmie

Wine   Mont...
Dom Per...

...oiled mushrooms
french beans
pop-overs
sliced tomatoes
vinaigrette → ce...
Ge...

Wines

...mtrachet
...urgundy
...e Perignon

Flowers

...et yellow roses—white
...e cloth

Gown & Jewels worn   Paisle...

Table Plan

Mr le P

Jim
Frances
Jim Jr
Nick
Free man

Gourmet's PARTIES

Gourmet's PARTIES

FROM THE EDITORS OF GOURMET

Photographs by Romulo A. Yanes

CONDÉ NAST BOOKS   RANDOM HOUSE
New York

Copyright © 1997 The Condé Nast Publications Inc. All rights reserved under International and Pan-American Copyright Conventions. Published in the United States by Random House, Inc., New York, and simultaneously in Canada by Random House of Canada Limited, Toronto.

LIBRARY OF CONGRESS CATALOGING-IN-PUBLICATION DATA

Main entry under title:
Gourmet's Parties/from the editors of Gourmet; food photographs by Romulo A. Yanes.
  p. cm.
  Includes index.
  ISBN 0-375-50030-8 (alk. paper)
  1. Cookery. 2. Entertaining.   I. Gourmet.
TX714.G682   1997   97-10665
642—dc21

Random House website address:
http://www.randomhouse.com/

Some of the recipes in this work were published previously in *Gourmet* Magazine.

Printed in the United States of America on acid-free paper.

98765432
First Edition

All informative text in this book was written by Diane Keitt and Caroline A. Schleifer.

Front Jacket: Coriander Lime Shrimp, page 96; Prosciutto-Wrapped Asparagus, page 58; Roasted Sweet Potato Bites, page 174; Indonesian Peanut Dip with Crudités, page 175; Stone Crab Claws with Parsley Sauce, page 175.

FOR CONDÉ NAST BOOKS

Jill Cohen, *President*
Ellen Maria Bruzelius, *Division Vice President*
Lucille Friedman, *Fulfillment Manager*
Tom Downing, *Direct Marketing Manager*
Jill Neal, *Direct Marketing Manager*
Jennifer Metz, *Direct Marketing Associate*
Paul DiNardo, *Direct Marketing Assistant*
Serafino J. Cambareri, *Quality Control Manager*

FOR GOURMET BOOKS

Diane Keitt, *Director*
Caroline A. Schleifer, *Associate Editor*

FOR GOURMET MAGAZINE

Gail Zweigenthal, *Editor-in-Chief*

Zanne Early Stewart, *Executive Food Editor*
Kemp Miles Minifie, *Senior Food Editor*
Alexis M. Touchet, *Associate Food Editor*
Amy Mastrangelo, *Food Editor*
Lori Walther, *Food Editor*
Elizabeth Vought, *Food Editor*
Katy Massam, *Food Editor*
Shelton Wiseman, *Food Editor*
Alix Palley, *Food Editor*

Romulo A. Yanes, *Photographer*
Marjorie H. Webb, *Style Director*
Nancy Purdum, *Senior Style Editor*

Produced in association with
MEDIA PROJECTS INCORPORATED

Carter Smith, *Executive Editor*
Anne B. Wright, *Project Editor*
John W. Kern, *Production Editor*
Marilyn Flaig, *Indexer*

Joel Avirom, *Jacket and Book Design*
Jason Snyder, *Design Assistant*

The text of this book was set in Fairfield and Venus by Joel Avirom. The four-color separations were done by The Color Company, Seiple Lithographers, and Applied Graphic Technologies. The book was printed and bound at R. R. Donnelley and Sons. Stock is Citation Web Gloss, Westvāco.

ACKNOWLEDGMENTS

The editors of Gourmet Books would like to thank everyone who contributed to *Gourmet's Parties*, especially Leslie Pendleton, who planned the menus and developed 120 new recipes; Alexis Touchet, Liz Vought, Lori Walther, and Shelley Wiseman, who diligently tested and perfected each recipe; and Zanne Stewart, who provided thoughtful guidance for this book.

Our photographer, Romulo Yanes, and stylists, Marjorie Webb and Nancy Purdum, merit special mention. Their cover photo, conceptualized by Joel Avirom, with food styled by Liz Vought, captures the essence of graceful entertaining. Additional photography by Lans Christensen, Julian Nieman, Mathias Oppersdorff, and John Vaughan further enhances our pages.

Gerald Asher, *Gourmet's* wine editor, selected wines with his usual *esprit*. Hobby McKenney, Kemp Minifie, Anne Wright, John Kern, and Sara Pomykacz answered wide-ranging questions and refined the manuscript at all stages. And, finally, we thank our designer, Joel Avirom, whose handsome design for this book inspires a fresh approach to planning parties.

RECIPE KEY

- Read through each recipe before beginning to cook.
- Measure liquids in glass or clear plastic liquid-measuring cups.
- Measure dry ingredients in dry-measuring cups that can be leveled off with a straight edge.
- Measure flour by spooning (not scooping) it into a dry-measuring cup and leveling off without tapping or shaking cup.
- Do not sift flour unless specified in recipe. When sifted four is called for, sift before measuring (even if label says "presifted").
- Measure skillets and baking pans across the top.
- Large eggs are labeled as such. Do not substitute extra-large or jumbo.
- Lettuces, greens, and herbs should be washed and dried before proceeding with recipe.

CONTENTS

Introduction 9

DINING ROOM PARTIES

KITCHEN PARTIES

GARDEN PARTIES

GETAWAY PARTIES

INTRODUCTION

Not so long ago, having a party meant polishing the silver and setting the dining room table for an elegant dinner. While everyone loves a fancy party now and then, lifestyles have changed, and so has the way we entertain. As *Gourmet's Parties* will show you, there are many options. You can have a few friends over for pasta in your kitchen; host a *fajitas* party on your patio; even organize a day of skiing followed by fondue. Thirty-eight party ideas are included, serving four to twenty-four. And, naturally, our food editors have thought of every detail.

Unlike other party-planning cookbooks, ours is arranged by location: dining room for more formal occasions; kitchen for relaxed gatherings; garden for *alfresco* feasts; and getaways for parties with away-from-home themes. All of the menus are designed with the ease of the host in mind. Many recipes can be made in 45 minutes or less, noted by a clock symbol ◐, and many more can be prepared ahead of time. (See make-ahead information on the menu pages and in italics within the recipes). Needless to say, it is nice to do as much as possible *before* your guests arrive.

Throughout the book, look for shortcuts that don't compromise flavor—just remember that quality is essential. We often call for store-bought breads (a wonderful bakery is worth a search); and occasionally we suggest a green salad without giving a recipe. Toss any fresh, crisp salad with a simple vinaigrette. Prepared items also are real time savers. Try frozen puff pastry topped with *tapenade* and sun-dried tomatoes (page 173) for one of our favorite hors d'oeuvres. And, when time is scarce and you need a quick dessert, our brown sugar sour cream topping (page 145) is delicious on any cut-up fresh fruit. Finally, we've included mail order sources (page 231) for difficult-to-find items.

When you stop to think about it, *Gourmet* magazine has been planning parties, every month, for over 50 years. Let us inspire you to host more of your own with *Gourmet's Parties*.

Gail Zweigenthal
Editor-in-Chief

1

DINING
ROOM
PARTIES

Perfectly elegant and sophisticated, our little New Year's menu promises a memorable evening. Although some specialty ingredients are required, everything except the pheasant and rolls can be purchased days ahead. When ordering pheasant from your butcher or by mail (page 231), ask for farm-raised female pheasants (hens), which are more tender and have better texture than male pheasants.

◆ Profiteroles: Ice cream may be made 1 week ahead (or serve store-bought). Sauce may be made 1 week ahead. Puffs may be baked 1 day ahead.

◆ Pheasant: Bird may be cut up and stock prepared 1 day ahead. Wild rice may be baked 1 day ahead.

SMOKED SALMON AND CUCUMBER CANAPÉS

Veuve Clicquot Réserve Brut Champagne 1989

BRAISED PHEASANT WITH RED CABBAGE WILD RICE

DINNER ROLLS (STORE-BOUGHT)

ENDIVE, RED-LEAF LETTUCE, AND STILTON SALAD

Burgess Napa Valley Vintage Select Cabernet Sauvignon 1993

CHOCOLATE PROFITEROLES WITH CARAMEL COFFEE ICE CREAM AND BITTERSWEET CHOCOLATE SAUCE

SERVES 4

AN INTIMATE NEW YEAR'S EVE

SMOKED SALMON AND CUCUMBER CANAPÉS

1 cucumber, peeled, seeded, and chopped

½ teaspoon salt

¼ pound sliced smoked salmon, chopped
　　coarse

2 tablespoons finely chopped red onion

1 tablespoon drained bottled small capers

¼ teaspoon freshly ground black pepper

¼ cup sour cream

1 tablespoon minced fresh dill

1 teaspoon drained bottled horseradish

twenty ¼-inch-thick bread rounds, cut from
　　a thin baguette and toasted lightly

2 tablespoons salmon roe

In a sieve set over a bowl toss cucumber with salt and drain 20 minutes. Rinse cucumber briefly and pat dry.

In another bowl stir together cucumber, salmon, onion, capers, and pepper until combined well. In a small bowl stir together sour cream, dill, and horseradish until combined well.

Divide salmon mixture among toasts and top with sour cream mixture and roe.

Makes 20 canapés.

BRAISED PHEASANT WITH RED CABBAGE WILD RICE

FOR WILD RICE

1 cup wild rice

2 cups chicken broth

2 tablespoons olive oil

8 bacon slices

1 large onion, sliced thin

4 cups thinly sliced red cabbage
　　(about ¼ head)

4 teaspoons red-wine vinegar

FOR PHEASANT

two 2-pound pheasants* (preferably hens,
　　which come with feet attached)

3 cups water

1 bay leaf

1 teaspoon salt

½ teaspoon black pepper

½ teaspoon ground allspice

3 tablespoons olive oil

bacon drippings reserved from making
　　wild rice

⅔ cup golden raisins

½ cup minced shallots (about 6)

½ cup gin

1 cup dry white wine

2 teaspoons tomato paste

*two 3-inch fresh rosemary sprigs plus
     1 teaspoon minced leaves*

1 cup halved seedless red and/or green grapes

** available at some butcher shops and by mail order
     (page 231)*

Make wild rice:

Preheat oven to 350° F.

In a fine sieve rinse wild rice well and drain. In a small saucepan bring broth to a simmer. In a 1½-quart flameproof casserole sauté rice in oil over moderately high heat, stirring, 1 minute and stir in hot broth and salt and pepper to taste. Bring mixture to a boil and bake, covered, in middle of oven 1 hour, or until liquid is absorbed and rice is tender. *Rice may be prepared up to this point 1 day ahead and chilled, covered. Reheat rice.*

While rice is baking, in a 12-inch skillet cook bacon over moderate heat until crisp and transfer to paper towels to drain. Transfer all but 2 tablespoons drippings to a small bowl and reserve for cooking pheasant. Heat drippings remaining in skillet over moderately high heat until hot but not smoking and sauté onion and cabbage, stirring, until softened. Add vinegar and salt and pepper to taste and sauté, stirring, 1 minute. Chop bacon. Just before serving, stir cabbage mixture and bacon into rice.

Make pheasant:

Rinse pheasants under cold water and pat dry inside and out. Cut each pheasant into 6 serving pieces, transferring feet, backs, necks,

and wing tips to a large saucepan. To saucepan add water and bay leaf and simmer, uncovered, 15 minutes, or until reduced to about 1½ cups. Pour stock through a fine sieve into a heatproof bowl.

In a cup stir together salt, pepper, and allspice. Pat pheasant dry again and sprinkle evenly with allspice mixture. In a large heavy skillet heat 1½ tablespoons oil with 1 tablespoon reserved drippings over moderately high heat until hot but not smoking. Sauté pheasant in batches until golden, about 5 minutes on each side, transferring to a platter and adding remaining 1½ tablespoons oil and up to 1 tablespoon reserved drippings.

In fat remaining in skillet cook raisins and shallots over moderate heat, stirring, until shallots are softened. Stir in gin and boil until most is evaporated. Stir in wine and boil until reduced by about half. Stir in stock, tomato paste, rosemary sprigs, and salt and pepper to taste and bring to a boil. Transfer sauce to a flameproof roasting pan large enough to hold pheasant in one layer.

To sauce add pheasant, skin sides down, and braise, tightly covered with foil, in middle of 350° F. oven until breast meat is cooked through and tender, about 10 minutes. Transfer breasts to a plate and keep warm, covered. Braise legs and thighs until cooked through and tender, about 10 minutes more. Transfer legs and thighs to plate and keep warm, covered. Stir minced rosemary and grapes into sauce and boil until slightly thickened, about 1 minute.

Serve pheasant with sauce and wild rice.

Serves 4.

Photo opposite

ENDIVE, RED-LEAF LETTUCE, AND STILTON SALAD

FOR VINAIGRETTE

> 1½ tablespoons Champagne vinegar
> or other white-wine vinegar
>
> 1 tablespoon mayonnaise
>
> 1 tablespoon medium-dry Sherry
>
> 1 teaspoon Dijon mustard
>
> ¼ cup extra-virgin olive oil
>
> 2 Belgian endives (about ¾ pound),
> cut crosswise into ½-inch-thick pieces
>
> 1 large head red leaf lettuce, torn into
> bite-size pieces (about 3 cups)
>
> ½ cup crumbled Stilton cheese (about
> 2 ounces)

Make vinaigrette:

In a small bowl whisk together vinegar, mayonnaise, Sherry, mustard, and salt and pepper to taste and add oil in a stream, whisking until emulsified.

In a large bowl toss endive and lettuce with vinaigrette and salt and pepper to taste.

Serve salad topped with Stilton.

Serves 4.

CHOCOLATE PROFITEROLES

FOR PROFITEROLES

> ½ cup all-purpose flour
>
> 2 tablespoons unsweetened cocoa powder
> (preferably Dutch-process)
>
> 3 tablespoons unsalted butter, cut into bits
>
> ½ cup plus 2 tablespoons water
>
> 1 tablespoon granulated sugar
>
> 2 large eggs
>
> caramel coffee ice cream (recipe follows)
> confectioners' sugar for dusting
> bittersweet chocolate sauce (page 17)

Make profiteroles:

Preheat oven to 400° F. and butter a large baking sheet.

Into a bowl sift together flour and cocoa powder. In a small heavy saucepan bring butter and water to a boil with sugar and a pinch of salt over high heat, stirring until butter is melted. Reduce heat to moderate. Add flour mixture all at once and cook, beating with a wooden spoon, until mixture pulls away from side of pan, forming a ball. Transfer mixture to a bowl and with an electric mixer on high speed beat in eggs, 1 at a time, beating well after each addition. Drop dough by rounded tablespoons onto baking sheet, forming 12 mounds.

Bake profiteroles in middle of oven 20 minutes, or until puffed and crisp, and cool on a rack. *Profiteroles may be made 1 day ahead and kept in an airtight container at room temperature. Reheat profiteroles on a baking sheet in a preheated 375° F. oven 5 minutes, or until crisp, and cool on rack before proceeding.*

With a serrated knife cut profiteroles in half horizontally. Discard any uncooked dough from centers and sandwich a small scoop (about 1½ inches in diameter) of ice cream between top and bottom of each profiterole. Dust profiteroles with confectioners' sugar. Pour about ¼ cup warm sauce onto each of 4 dessert plates and arrange 3 profiteroles on sauce.

Makes 12 profiteroles, serving 4.

Photo on page 12

CARAMEL COFFEE ICE CREAM

1½ *cups milk*

1½ *cups heavy cream*

¼ *cup coffee beans, crushed lightly*

1 *vanilla bean, split lengthwise*

⅔ *cup plus 3 tablespoons sugar*

3 *tablespoons water*

5 *large egg yolks*

In a saucepan bring milk and 1 cup cream just to a boil with coffee beans and vanilla bean and remove pan from heat. Steep coffee mixture, covered, 30 minutes.

While coffee mixture is steeping, in a small heavy saucepan cook ⅔ cup sugar and water over moderate heat until sugar begins to melt and continue to cook, stirring with a fork and swirling pan, until a deep golden caramel. Remove pan from heat and carefully add remaining ½ cup cream down side of pan

(mixture will bubble up), whisking until smooth. Cool caramel.

Have ready a large bowl of ice and cold water. In a bowl whisk together yolks, remaining 3 tablespoons sugar, and a pinch salt and add coffee mixture in a stream, whisking. Transfer custard to a heavy saucepan and cook over moderately low heat, stirring, until thickened and registers 170° F. on a candy thermometer. Remove pan from heat and whisk in caramel mixture. Pour custard through a fine sieve into a metal bowl and set in bowl of ice water. Stir custard until cold and freeze in an ice-cream maker. Transfer ice cream to a 1-quart container and freeze until firm. *Ice cream may be made 1 week ahead.*

Makes about 1 quart.

BITTERSWEET CHOCOLATE SAUCE

6 *ounces fine-quality bittersweet chocolate (not unsweetened), chopped*

3 *tablespoons water*

¼ *cup heavy cream*

2 *tablespoons Kahlúa or other coffee-flavored liqueur, or to taste*

In a metal bowl set over a saucepan of simmering water melt chocolate with water and cream, stirring until smooth, and stir in Kahlúa. *Sauce may be made 1 week ahead and chilled, covered. Reheat sauce in metal bowl over simmering water.*

Makes about 1 cup.

On Sunday afternoons, French families gather at home or at a bistro for an unhurried meal. Our lunch, filled with regional favorites from Burgundy (the stew) to the Loire Valley (the desserts), is hearty and simple to prepare. And yet, these dishes—like the French themselves—are quite stylish: a swirl of cream decorates the soup; a sprinkle of chopped parsley and a handful of fresh sprigs adorn the stew; and on the

custards, crystallized violets and a puff of whipped cream make a lasting impression.

♦ Soup and croutons may be made 1 day ahead.

♦ Short ribs improve if made 1 day ahead.

♦ Shallots for the mashed potatoes may be fried 1 day ahead.

♦ Custards must be chilled at least 4 hours and up to 1 day.

♦ Macaroons and filling may be made 1 day ahead.

FRESH PEA SOUP

BURGUNDY-BRAISED SHORT RIBS
AND VEGETABLES

MASHED POTATOES
WITH FRIED SHALLOTS

GREEN SALAD

*Joseph Phelps Le Mistral
Napa Valley Red Wine 1994*

CHOCOLATE CUSTARDS

CHOCOLATE MACAROONS

Antinori Muffato della Sala 1994

SERVES 6

SUNDAY BISTRO LUNCH

FRESH PEA SOUP

===

FOR CROUTONS

 *1½ cups ½-inch cubes French or Italian
 bread*

 2 tablespoons unsalted butter, melted

FOR SOUP

 *2 leeks (white and pale green parts only),
 chopped, washed well, and drained*

 2 tablespoons unsalted butter

 3 cups chicken broth

 2 cups water

 4 cups shelled fresh or frozen peas

 4 cups chopped lettuce

 ½ cup fresh mint leaves

 GARNISH: *¼ cup chilled heavy cream*

Make croutons:

 Preheat oven to 350° F.

 In a bowl drizzle bread cubes with butter,
tossing to coat well, and spread in a shallow
baking dish. Bake bread cubes in middle of
oven, stirring occasionally, 10 minutes, or
until lightly golden and crisp. Season croutons with salt. *Croutons may be made 1 day
ahead and kept in an airtight container at
room temperature.*

Make soup:

 In a large saucepan cook leeks in butter
over moderately low heat, stirring occasionally, until softened. Add broth and water and
bring to a boil. Add peas and lettuce and
simmer, partially covered, until peas are tender, about 10 minutes. Stir in mint and in

a blender or food processor purée soup in
batches, transferring to a bowl. (Use caution
when blending hot liquids.) *Soup may be
made 1 day ahead and chilled, covered.*
Return soup to pan and season with salt and
pepper. Reheat soup over moderately low
heat, stirring, until heated through.

 In a small bowl beat cream until slightly
thickened but still pourable and season with
salt. Ladle soup into 6 bowls. Spoon several
drops of cream onto each serving and draw a
skewer or knife through drops to form decorative patterns. Serve soup with croutons.

 *Makes about 8 cups, serving 6 as a first
course.*

Photo on page 18

BURGUNDY-BRAISED
SHORT RIBS AND
VEGETABLES

===

*4 pounds beef short ribs (sometimes called
 Flanken)*

3 tablespoons vegetable oil

2 cups beef broth

1 cup dry red wine (preferably Burgundy)

1 teaspoon dried thyme, crumbled

1 bay leaf

*1 pound carrots, cut into 3-inch lengths,
 halved lengthwise if thick*

1 pound small white mushrooms, trimmed

*1 pound small white onions, peeled and
 halved lengthwise*

4 garlic cloves, chopped coarse

2 tablespoons all-purpose flour

2 tablespoons minced fresh parsley leaves

GARNISH: *fresh parsley sprigs*

Pat short ribs dry and season with salt and pepper. In a large heavy kettle heat oil over moderately high heat until hot but not smoking and brown ribs in batches, transferring with tongs to a platter. Pour off fat from kettle. In kettle bring broth, wine, thyme, bay leaf, and ribs to a boil and simmer, covered tightly, 1 1/2 hours. Add carrots, mushrooms, onions, and garlic and simmer, covered, 1 hour, or until meat and vegetables are tender.

Transfer meat, discarding any bones and gristle that separate from it, and vegetables with a slotted spoon to a large bowl and keep warm, covered. Skim fat from braising liquid in kettle. In a small bowl whisk together 1/4 cup braising liquid and flour until smooth and add to remaining braising liquid. Bring mixture to a boil, whisking, and simmer until sauce is thickened, about 5 minutes. Season sauce with salt and pepper and add ribs and vegetables. *Stew improves in flavor if made 1 day ahead and cooled, uncovered, before being chilled, covered.* Heat stew over moderate heat, stirring occasionally, until heated through.

Serve stew sprinkled with minced parsley and garnished with parsley sprigs.

Serves 6.

MASHED POTATOES WITH FRIED SHALLOTS

vegetable oil for frying

12 shallots, sliced thin crosswise

4 1/2 pounds russet (baking) potatoes (about 8 large)

1 stick (1/2 cup) unsalted butter, softened

In a large saucepan heat 1/2 inch oil over moderately high heat until hot but not smoking and fry shallots in batches, until golden and crisp, transferring with a slotted spoon to a large bowl. *Shallots may be fried 1 day ahead and cooled before being kept in an airtight container at room temperature.*

Peel and halve potatoes and in a kettle cover with cold water by 2 inches. Bring to a boil and simmer 30 minutes, or until potatoes are very tender. Reserve 1 cup cooking water and drain potatoes. Force potatoes through a ricer or a food mill fitted with coarse disk into bowl of shallots. Stir in butter and enough reserved cooking water to reach desired consistency and season with salt and pepper.

Serves 8.

CHOCOLATE CUSTARDS

—

1 cup milk

*3 ounces fine-quality bittersweet chocolate
(not unsweetened), chopped fine*

½ teaspoon vanilla

3 large egg yolks

¼ cup sugar

GARNISH: *whipped cream and crystallized
violets**

** available at some specialty foods shops and by mail
order (page 231)*

Preheat oven to 400° F.

In a small heavy saucepan heat milk and
chocolate over moderate heat, whisking occasionally, until chocolate is melted and mixture
just comes to a boil. Stir in vanilla and remove
pan from heat. In a heatproof bowl whisk
together yolks and sugar until combined well
and add chocolate mixture in a slow stream,
whisking. Pour custard through a very fine
sieve into a 2-cup measure or pitcher.

Divide custard among six ¼-cup ramekins
and cover each with foil. Put ramekins in a
baking pan and add enough hot water to pan
to reach halfway up sides of ramekins.

Bake custards in middle of oven 25 minutes, or until just set. Transfer ramekins to a
rack and cool, covered. *Chill custards, covered, at least 4 hours and up to 1 day.*

Serve custards garnished with whipped
cream and candied violets.

Serves 6.

Photo opposite

CHOCOLATE MACAROONS

—

FOR MACAROONS

*⅔ cup blanched whole almonds (about
4 ounces)*

1¾ cups confectioners' sugar

*¼ cup unsweetened Dutch-process cocoa
powder*

3 large egg whites

1 tablespoon granulated sugar

FOR FILLING

⅓ cup heavy cream

1 teaspoon milk

*2 tablespoons unsweetened Dutch-process
cocoa powder*

*4 ounces fine-quality bittersweet chocolate
(not unsweetened), chopped*

7 tablespoons unsalted butter, cut into pieces

Make macaroons:

Preheat oven to 400° F. and line 2 large
baking sheets with parchment paper.

In a food processor grind almonds with
1 cup confectioners' sugar until finely ground.
Add cocoa powder and remaining ¾ cup
confectioners' sugar and blend well. In a large
bowl with an electric mixer beat whites with a
pinch salt until they just hold soft peaks. Add
granulated sugar, beating until meringue
holds stiff, glossy peaks. Fold in almond mixture gently but thoroughly and transfer to a
large pastry bag fitted with ½-inch plain tip.

Pipe about 25 small mounds (1 inch in
diameter) 2 inches apart on each baking
sheet. Bake macaroons in middle and upper

thirds of oven 8 minutes, or until tops appear dry but macaroons are still slightly soft to the touch. Transfer macaroons on parchment paper to dampened kitchen towels and cool 5 minutes. Carefully peel macaroons off parchment paper and cool completely on racks. *Macaroons may be made 1 day ahead and kept in layers separated by wax paper in an airtight container, chilled.*

Make filling:

In a saucepan bring cream and milk just to a boil and whisk in cocoa powder. Remove pan from heat and stir in chopped chocolate and butter until smooth. Cool filling and chill 30 minutes, or until firm enough to hold its shape when piped or spread. *Filling may be made 1 day ahead and chilled, covered.*

Spread filling generously on flat side of half of macaroons with a knife or small metal spatula. Top filling with remaining macaroons, flat sides down, to form sandwiches.

Makes about 25 macaroon sandwiches.

Photo below

As the days grow shorter, our harvest feast satisfies autumnal cravings with comforting dishes and cozy heartland touches. You'll need 4 tenderloins for the pork roulades—look for them in cryovac packages at your supermarket (usually 2 per pack). To save time, ask the butcher to butterfly and flatten them for you. Buy cut-up, peeled squash for another shortcut.

◆ Spread may be made 1 week ahead.

◆ Dessert: Ice cream may be made 1 week ahead (or serve store-bought). Cake may be made 1 day ahead.

◆ Vinaigrette for salad may be made 1 day ahead.

◆ Scalloped potatoes may be baked 1 hour ahead and reheated.

AUTUMN HARVEST FEAST

CHEDDAR SPREAD

½ pound extra-sharp yellow Cheddar, grated
coarse (about 3 cups)

¼ pound extra-sharp white Cheddar, grated
coarse (about 1½ cups)

3 celery ribs, chopped fine (about 1 cup)

1 medium red onion, chopped fine (about
¾ cup)

¾ cup mayonnaise

2½ teaspoons Dijon mustard

1½ teaspoons drained bottled horseradish

ACCOMPANIMENT: *salted crackers*

In a bowl toss together Cheddars, celery, and
onion and stir in remaining ingredients and
pepper to taste until combined well. *Spread
keeps, covered and chilled, 1 week.*

Serve spread with crackers.

Makes about 3 cups.

PORK TENDERLOIN AND SPINACH ROULADES

2 cups chopped onion

4 garlic cloves, minced

3 tablespoons vegetable oil

2 pounds fresh spinach (about 2 bunches),
washed well, coarse stems discarded,
and leaves chopped coarse

2 teaspoons minced fresh thyme leaves

4 whole pork tenderloins (about 4 pounds
total)

1 teaspoon minced fresh lemon zest
(removed with a vegetable peeler)

1½ cups freshly grated Parmesan
(about 4 ounces)

⅓ cup dry white wine

1⅓ cups water

Preheat oven to 350° F.

In a large skillet cook onion and garlic in
1 tablespoon oil over moderate heat, stirring,
until golden. Add spinach and thyme and
cook, stirring, until spinach is wilted, about 3
minutes. Transfer mixture to a bowl and cool.

With a sharp knife make a lengthwise cut
down center of 1 pork tenderloin, two-thirds of
the way through. Press tenderloin open and
arrange, cut side up, between 2 sheets of plastic
wrap. Gently pound tenderloin until flattened
into a rectangle about ⅓ inch thick. Repeat
procedure with remaining 3 tenderloins. Peel
away enough plastic wrap from 2 tenderloins to
overlap 2 long sides by 1 inch and gently pound
tenderloins together to form an even thickness.
Repeat procedure with remaining 2 tenderloins.

Into cooled spinach mixture stir zest, Parmesan, and salt and pepper to taste until combined well. Discard top sheets of plastic wrap from pork rectangles and divide filling between them, spreading it evenly and leaving a 1-inch border on all sides. Beginning with a long side and using plastic wrap as a guide, roll up pork jelly-roll fashion. Discard plastic wrap and tie *roulades* tightly at 1-inch intervals with kitchen string.

Pat *roulades* dry and season with salt and pepper. In a large heavy skillet heat remaining 2 tablespoons oil over moderately high heat until hot but not smoking and brown *roulades,* 1 at a time, on all sides, transferring to a large roasting pan.

Roast *roulades* in middle of oven 50 minutes, or to 160° F. on an instant-read meat thermometer. Transfer *roulades* to a cutting board and let stand, covered loosely with foil, 10 minutes.

Add wine to roasting pan and deglaze over high heat, scraping up brown bits. Add water and boil gravy until reduced to about 1 cup. Discard strings from *roulades* and cut pork into ¹/₂-inch-thick slices.

Pour gravy onto a heated platter and arrange *roulades* on it.

Serves 6.

Photo on page 26

MIXED GREEN SALAD WITH CIDER VINAIGRETTE

1 shallot, minced

2 teaspoons Dijon mustard

3 tablespoons apple cider

2 tablespoons cider vinegar

¼ cup vegetable oil

12 cups torn mixed salad greens (such as red leaf lettuce, radicchio, and romaine)

2 bacon slices, cooked and crumbled

In a bowl whisk together shallot, mustard, cider, vinegar, oil and salt and pepper to taste until combined well. *Vinaigrette may be made 1 day ahead and chilled, covered. Whisk vinaigrette before using.*

In a large bowl toss greens with vinaigrette until coated well.

Serve salad sprinkled with bacon.

Serves 6.

SCALLOPED POTATOES AND BUTTERNUT SQUASH WITH LEEKS

—

3 cups thinly sliced leeks (about 6 large,
    white and pale green parts only),
    washed well and drained

1 stick (½ cup) unsalted butter

3½ cups milk

6 tablespoons all-purpose flour

1½ pounds boiling potatoes (about 4 large)

1 pound butternut squash, quartered, seeded,
    peeled, and cut into ⅛-inch-thick slices

1½ cups coarsely grated Gruyère (about 4
    ounces)

Preheat oven to 400° F. and generously butter
a 3-quart gratin dish (at least 2 inches deep).

In a skillet cook leeks in 3 tablespoons
butter over moderately low heat, stirring, until
very soft.

In a saucepan bring milk just to a boil.
In a heavy saucepan melt remaining 5 tablespoons butter over moderately low heat. Whisk
in flour and cook *roux*, whisking, 3 minutes.
Add milk in a stream, whisking, and bring to
a boil. Simmer sauce, whisking, 1 minute,
or until thickened, and season with salt and
pepper.

Peel potatoes and slice ⅛ inch thick.
Spread about one third sauce in gratin dish
and cover with one third potato and squash
slices, overlapping them slightly. Cover slices
with one third leeks and sprinkle with one
third Gruyère. Make 2 more layers with sauce,
potatoes and squash, leeks, and Gruyère in
same manner.

Bake gratin, covered with foil, in middle
of oven 20 minutes. Remove foil and bake 30
minutes more, or until top is golden and vegetables are tender. *Gratin may be made 1 hour
ahead and kept at room temperature. Reheat
gratin in 350° F. oven while preparing gravy
for roulades (recipe on page 26).*

Serves 6.

DATE PECAN PUMPKIN SQUARES

—

2½ cups all-purpose flour

1½ teaspoons baking powder

¾ teaspoon cinnamon

½ teaspoon freshly grated nutmeg

½ teaspoon ground cloves

½ teaspoon salt

1 pound pitted dried dates, cut into thirds
    (about 2 cups)

2 sticks (1 cup) plus 2 tablespoons unsalted
    butter, softened

2 cups packed light brown sugar

2 large eggs

1 cup canned solid-pack pumpkin

1 teaspoon vanilla

¼ cup water

1½ cups chopped pecans

ACCOMPANIMENTS:

nutmeg ice cream (recipe follows)

bourbon burnt sugar sauce (page 29)

Preheat oven to 350° F. and grease a 13- by 9- by 2-inch baking pan.

Into a bowl sift together flour, baking powder, spices, and salt. In a small bowl toss dates with ¼ cup flour mixture until well coated. In another bowl with an electric mixer beat together butter and brown sugar until light and fluffy. Add eggs, 1 at a time, beating well after each addition, and beat in pumpkin, vanilla, and water. With mixer on low speed gradually beat in remaining flour mixture and stir in date mixture and pecans until batter is combined well.

Pour batter into baking pan and bake in middle of oven 1 hour, or until a tester comes out clean. Cool cake in pan on a rack. *Cake may be made 1 day ahead and kept, covered, at room temperature.*

Cut cake into 12 squares and serve with ice cream and warm sauce.

Makes 12 squares, serving 6 generously.

Photo on page 24

NUTMEG ICE CREAM

1½ cups milk
1½ cups heavy cream
3 large eggs
¾ cup sugar
1 teaspoon freshly grated nutmeg
⅛ teaspoon salt
¼ teaspoon vanilla

Have ready a large bowl of ice and cold water. In a heavy saucepan bring milk and heavy cream just to a boil. In a bowl whisk together eggs, sugar, nutmeg, salt, and vanilla until combined well. Add ½ cup milk mixture in a stream, whisking, and whisk egg mixture into remaining milk mixture. Cook custard over moderate heat, stirring constantly with a wooden spatula, until it thickens and registers 175° F. on a candy thermometer (do not boil).

Transfer custard to a metal bowl set in bowl of ice water. Stir custard until cold and freeze in an ice-cream maker. Transfer ice cream to a 1-quart container and freeze until firm. *Ice cream keeps 1 week.*

Makes about 1 quart.

BOURBON BURNT SUGAR SAUCE

1½ cups sugar
½ cup hot water
⅓ cup bourbon

In a large deep heavy skillet cook sugar over moderate heat until it begins to melt and continue to cook, stirring with a fork and swirling skillet, until a golden caramel.

Remove skillet from heat and carefully add hot water down side of skillet (mixture will steam and caramel will harden). Cook mixture over moderate heat, stirring, until caramel is dissolved. Add bourbon and simmer 2 minutes. Remove skillet from heat and cool sauce slightly (it will thicken as it cools).

Makes about 1½ cups.

ROASTED VEGETABLE NAPOLEONS

BRAISED CHICKEN WITH FENNEL,
OLIVES, AND SAFFRON

HERBED ORZO AND PEAS

MESCLUN AND FRISÉE
WITH ORANGE VINAIGRETTE

CRUSTY BREAD (STORE-BOUGHT)

*Ferrari-Carano
Sonoma County Fumé Blanc 1995*

LEMON ROSEMARY CUSTARD CAKES

*Château Ste. Michelle Columbia Valley
Washington State Late Harvest
White Riesling Horse Heaven Vineyard 1995*

SERVES 6

Dramatic presentations, such as our towering vegetable napoleons and dainty little lemon custard cakes in individual cups, will impress new neighbors and old friends alike. Although the napoleons look very structured, feel free to layer the vegetables any way you like. Unusual ingredients also add interest to the menu: a pinch of saffron threads colors the braised chicken a vibrant gold (avoid saffron powder); orzo (a rice-shaped pasta) offers an appealing alternative to rice pilaf; and a combination of mesclun (mixed baby greens) and frisée (curly endive) offer color and bite.

◆ Napoleons: Vegetables may be roasted 1 day ahead.

A WELCOMING
DINNER

ROASTED VEGETABLE NAPOLEONS

½ cup olive oil

1 pound eggplant, cut crosswise into
⅓-inch-thick slices

1 pound medium red potatoes, cut into
⅓-inch-thick slices

1¼ pounds zucchini, cut crosswise into
⅓-inch-thick slices

2 medium red onions, cut crosswise into
⅓-inch-thick slices

4 large plum tomatoes (about 1¼ pounds
total), cut lengthwise into ⅓-inch-thick
slices

¾ cup ricotta

1½ teaspoons chopped fresh thyme leaves

½ pound fresh mozzarella, cut into six
¼-inch-thick slices

6 fresh rosemary sprigs

Preheat oven to 450° F. and brush 2 baking sheets with some oil.

Arrange as many vegetables as possible in one layer on baking sheets. Brush vegetables with some oil and season with salt and pepper. Roast vegetables in middle and lower thirds of oven, switching position of sheets in oven halfway through roasting, until just tender and lightly browned, about 10 minutes. Transfer vegetables as roasted to a tray, arranging them in one layer. Roast remaining vegetables in same manner. *Vegetables may be roasted 1 day ahead and cooled completely before being chilled, layered between sheets of plastic wrap on trays and covered. Bring vegetables to room temperature before proceeding.*

In a small bowl stir together ricotta, thyme, and salt and pepper to taste.

Put 1 eggplant slice on a lightly oiled baking sheet. Spread 1 tablespoon ricotta mixture over eggplant. Cover ricotta mixture with 2 potato slices and layer with 2 zucchini slices, 1 onion slice, 1 mozzarella slice, 2 to 3 tomato slices, 2 zucchini slices, and 1 onion slice. Spread 1 tablespoon ricotta mixture over onion and top with 1 eggplant slice. Make 5 more napoleons using remaining vegetables, ricotta mixture, and mozzarella in same manner.

Insert a metal or wooden skewer through center of each napoleon to make a hole from top to bottom. Trim rosemary sprigs to 1 inch taller than napoleons and remove bottom leaves from each sprig, leaving about 1 inch of leaves around top. Insert 1 sprig into each napoleon and bake in middle of oven until mozzarella is melted and vegetables are heated through, about 5 minutes.

Serves 6.

Photo on page 30

Braised Chicken with Fennel, Olives, and Saffron

3 chicken breast halves (with skin and bones, about 1½ pounds total)

6 chicken thighs

1 tablespoon olive oil

1 large onion, chopped

2 garlic cloves, minced

1 fennel bulb (sometimes called anise), stalks trimmed flush with bulb and bulb halved lengthwise and sliced thin crosswise

1½ cups chicken broth

¼ cup fresh lemon juice

1 cup pimiento-stuffed green olives

scant ¼ teaspoon crumbled saffron

2 tablespoons all-purpose flour

2 tablespoons minced fresh parsley leaves

Preheat oven to 350° F.

Cut each chicken breast half crosswise in half (6 pieces total). Pat chicken breasts and thighs dry and season with salt and pepper. In a heavy kettle heat oil over moderately high heat until hot but not smoking and brown chicken in batches, transferring with tongs to a plate. Add onion and garlic to kettle and cook over moderately low heat, stirring, until vegetables begin to turn golden. Add fennel and cook, stirring, 5 minutes, or until slightly softened. Return chicken and any juices that have accumulated on plate to kettle and add broth, lemon juice, olives, and saffron. Bring mixture to a boil.

Braise chicken, covered, in middle of oven 35 minutes, or until tender. Return kettle to top of stove. Transfer ¼ cup cooking liquid to a heatproof bowl and whisk in flour until smooth. Stir flour mixture into chicken mixture and simmer, stirring, 2 minutes, or until sauce is thickened.

Serve chicken and vegetables sprinkled with parsley.

Serves 6.

HERBED ORZO AND PEAS

2 cups orzo (rice-shaped pasta,
    about ¾ pound)

2 cups fresh or frozen peas

3 tablespoons unsalted butter, softened

3 tablespoons minced fresh parsley leaves,
    or to taste

1 tablespoon minced fresh tarragon leaves,
    or to taste

3 tablespoons minced fresh chives

Bring a kettle of salted water to a boil and cook *orzo* 5 minutes. Add peas and boil 3 minutes, or until *orzo* is *al dente*. Drain *orzo* and peas well in a large sieve and transfer to a bowl. Stir in butter, herbs, and salt and pepper to taste, tossing until combined well.

Serves 6.

MESCLUN AND FRISÉE WITH ORANGE VINAIGRETTE

2 tablespoons white-wine vinegar

1 tablespoon fresh orange juice

2 shallots, halved lengthwise and sliced thin
    crosswise

¼ cup extra-virgin olive oil

1 head frisée* (French curly endive),
    torn into pieces

4 to 6 ounces mesclun (mixed baby greens,
    4 to 6 cups loosely packed)

*available at specialty produce markets and some
    supermarkets

In a small bowl whisk together vinegar, orange juice, shallots, and salt and pepper to taste and add oil in a stream, whisking until emulsified. In a large bowl toss greens with vinaigrette until coated well.

Serves 6.

TO WASH AND STORE SALAD GREENS

To Wash:
Immerse salad greens in a basin filled with cold water and swirl them around, allowing sand and dirt to come out of greens. Lift greens out of water, leaving grit behind, and shake off any excess. Dry greens well by either spinning in a salad spinner or patting between paper towels.

To Store:
Layer greens between dampened paper towels and keep in a well-sealed plastic bag in the refrigerator. Delicate greens, such as mesclun, mâche, and frisée may be kept for 2 days. Sturdy greens such as romaine, Bibb lettuce, and red lettuce may be kept for 4 days.

LEMON ROSEMARY
CUSTARD CAKES

——

3 large eggs, separated

1½ cups milk

1½ tablespoons unsalted butter, softened

¾ cup granulated sugar

¼ cup all-purpose flour

5 tablespoons fresh lemon juice

2 teaspoons freshly grated lemon zest

1 teaspoon minced fresh rosemary leaves

confectioners' sugar for dusting

GARNISH: fresh rosemary sprigs and/or
    crystallized violets*

*available at some specialty foods shops and by mail
    order (see page 231)

Preheat oven to 350° F. and lightly butter six 6-ounce ramekins.

In a small bowl whisk together yolks and milk. In a bowl with an electric mixer beat together butter and granulated sugar until combined well. Beat in flour, lemon juice, zest, rosemary, and a pinch salt. Add yolk mixture, beating until smooth.

In another bowl with cleaned beaters beat whites until they just hold stiff peaks and whisk about one third whites into lemon mixture to lighten. Fold in remaining whites gently but thoroughly.

Divide batter among ramekins and put ramekins in a baking pan. Pour enough hot water into pan to reach halfway up sides of ramekins and bake cakes in middle of oven 45 minutes. (Cake will rise to top and custard will remain on bottom of ramekins.)

Dust cakes with confectioners' sugar and garnish with rosemary sprigs and/or crystallized violets.

Serves 6.

Photo above

POTATO, PEA, AND CUMIN FRITTERS
WITH SPICY MINT SAUCE

CORIANDER-HONEY CHICKEN WITH
SWEET-AND-SOUR PEANUT SAUCE

HERBED LENTIL AND RICE SALAD

ROASTED CAULIFLOWER
WITH SCALLION AND LEMON

SPICED MANGO BREAD PUDDING

*Rheingau Riesling
Freiherr zu Knyphausen 1995*

SERVES 6

Even before your guests sit down to this South Asian inspired dinner, they will be intrigued by the fragrant aromas of potent spices: curry powder and whole cumin seeds for the fritters; coriander, turmeric, and cayenne for the chicken; and ginger, cinnamon, allspice, and cardamom for the bread pudding. Use only the freshest spices—ground spices, in particular, lose most of their pungency after 1 year. Buy small amounts from shops with frequent turnover, such as Indian markets, or use mail order (page 231).

- Bread pudding may be assembled 12 hours ahead.
- Herbed Lentil and Rice Salad may be prepared, in part, 1 day ahead.
- Chicken must marinate 2 hours.

SPICE UP YOUR WINTER DINNER

POTATO, PEA, AND CUMIN FRITTERS WITH SPICY MINT SAUCE

FOR FRITTER BATTER
> 3 russet (baking) potatoes
> (about 1½ pounds)
>
> 2 tablespoons grated onion
>
> ¾ teaspoon salt
>
> 2 tablespoons all-purpose flour
>
> 1 large egg
>
> 1 cup thawed frozen petit pois
> (small green peas)
>
> ¾ teaspoon cumin seeds, toasted
>
> ¼ cup freshly grated Parmesan
>
> 2 teaspoons curry powder

FOR SAUCE
> ¼ cup minced fresh mint or parsley leaves
>
> 2 tablespoons fresh lemon juice
>
> 1 tablespoon water
>
> 1 red or green fresh chili such as serrano or
> jalapeño, seeded and minced (wear
> rubber gloves)
>
> 1 teaspoon minced garlic
>
> vegetable oil for frying

Make fritter batter:

Peel potatoes and cut into chunks. In a food processor purée potatoes with onion and salt. Transfer purée to a large fine sieve set over a bowl and drain 10 minutes. Pour off liquid in bowl, leaving potato starch in bottom of bowl, and add potato purée and remaining batter ingredients to bowl, scraping starch up from bottom of bowl and stirring until combined well.

Make sauce:

In a bowl stir together sauce ingredients until combined well and season with salt.

Preheat oven to 200° F.

In a large skillet heat ¼ inch oil over moderately high heat until hot but not smoking. Working in batches, drop in fritter batter by rounded teaspoons, patting mounds into small pancakes with back of spoon, and fry 2 minutes on each side, or until browned and crisp. (Use caution as peas may "pop".) Transfer fritters as cooked to paper towels to drain and keep warm on a baking sheet in warm oven.

Serve fritters drizzled with sauce.

Makes about 60 fritters, serving 6 as an hors d'oeuvre.

CORIANDER-HONEY CHICKEN WITH SWEET-AND-SOUR PEANUT SAUCE

===

4 pounds chicken parts with skin and bones,
 breasts halved if whole and legs cut into
 drumstick and thigh sections

6 tablespoons soy sauce

1 tablespoon honey

1 tablespoon ground coriander seeds

1 to 2 garlic cloves, or to taste, minced and
 mashed to a paste with ½ teaspoon salt

2 teaspoons finely grated peeled fresh
 gingerroot

¼ teaspoon turmeric

¼ teaspoon cayenne, or to taste

ACCOMPANIMENT: *sweet-and-sour peanut sauce
 (recipe follows)*

Cut each breast half crosswise into 2 pieces
and cut 2 parallel diagonal slits on meat side
of each drumstick, thigh, and breast piece,
cutting through to bone (do not cut through
an edge).

In a large bowl whisk together remaining
ingredients and add chicken, turning to coat.
*Marinate chicken, covered and chilled, turning
occasionally, 2 hours.*

Preheat broiler and oil rack of broiler pan.

Arrange chicken pieces, skin sides down,
on rack of broiler pan, reserving marinade.
Broil chicken about 6 inches from heat,

turning over and basting with marinade
halfway through broiling, until golden brown
and cooked through, about 12 minutes.
(Breast pieces may be fully cooked before
drumsticks and thighs.) Discard any unused
marinade.

Serve chicken with peanut sauce.

Serves 6.

Photo on page 36

SWEET-AND-SOUR PEANUT SAUCE

 ===

¼ cup creamy or chunky peanut butter
 (preferably natural)

¼ cup soy sauce

2 tablespoons fresh lemon juice

1 tablespoon packed brown sugar

1½ teaspoons cayenne

GARNISH: *fresh coriander sprig*

In a small bowl whisk together all ingredients
until combined well.

Serve sauce garnished with coriander.

Makes about ⅔ cup.

HERBED LENTIL AND RICE SALAD

½ cup chopped onion

1 tablespoon vegetable oil

1 cup long-grain rice

2 cups water

1 teaspoon salt

1 cup lentils, picked over and rinsed

½ cup packed fresh flat-leafed parsley leaves, chopped

½ cup packed fresh mint leaves, chopped

1 garlic clove, minced

1 tablespoon rice vinegar (not seasoned)

1 cup vine-ripened cherry tomatoes, halved

In a 2-quart saucepan with a tight-fitting lid cook onion in oil, uncovered, over moderate heat, stirring, until golden brown. Add rice and stir until coated with oil. Add water and salt and boil, uncovered, stirring occasionally, until surface is covered with steam holes and grains on top appear dry. Reduce heat as much as possible and cover pan with lid. Cook rice 15 minutes more. Remove pan from heat and let rice stand, covered, 5 minutes.

While rice is cooking, to a large saucepan of salted water add lentils and bring to a boil. Cook lentils at a bare simmer until just tender, about 15 minutes. In a sieve rinse and drain lentils. Transfer rice to a bowl and fluff with a fork. Add lentils, tossing to combine

well. *Salad may be prepared up to this point 1 day ahead and cooled completely before being chilled, covered. If serving salad warm, reheat lentils and rice before proceeding.*

To salad add remaining ingredients and salt and pepper to taste and toss well. Serve salad warm or at room temperature.

Serves 6.

ROASTED CAULIFLOWER WITH SCALLION AND LEMON

3 pounds cauliflower (about 1½ heads), cut into 1-inch flowerets

2 tablespoons olive oil

¼ cup thinly sliced scallion

1 teaspoon finely grated fresh lemon zest

1 tablespoon fresh lemon juice, or to taste

Preheat oven to 500° F.

In a large shallow baking pan toss cauliflower with oil and salt and pepper to taste until coated well and roast in middle of oven 10 minutes. Stir in remaining ingredients and roast 2 to 5 minutes, or until cauliflower is browned in spots and tender.

Serves 6.

SPICED MANGO BREAD PUDDING

2 ripe mangoes (½ to ¾ pound each)

4 cups 1-inch cubes French or Italian bread

2¼ cups milk

2 whole large eggs plus 1 large egg yolk

½ cup plus 1 tablespoon sugar

2 teaspoons vanilla

¼ teaspoon ground cinnamon

¼ teaspoon ground ginger

⅛ teaspoon ground allspice

⅛ teaspoon ground cardamom

a pinch salt

1 tablespoon unsalted butter, cut into bits

ACCOMPANIMENT: *vanilla frozen yogurt*

Preheat oven to 375° F.

Standing 1 mango upright, cut a lengthwise slice, 1 inch thick, from a broad side of mango pit. Cut remaining broad side and remaining mango in same manner. With tip of a sharp knife score flesh in a cross-hatch pattern to form 1-inch cubes, being careful not to cut through skin. Push from skin side to turn each mango piece inside out and cut cubes of fruit away from skin. In a 9-inch square baking dish toss together mango and bread cubes.

In a small saucepan bring milk just to a boil and remove pan from heat. In a bowl whisk together eggs, yolk, ½ cup sugar, vanilla, spices, and salt and whisk in hot milk in a stream. Pour custard over bread mixture and let stand 5 minutes, or until liquid is absorbed. *Pudding may be prepared up to this point 12 hours ahead and chilled, covered.*

Sprinkle top of pudding with remaining tablespoon sugar and dot with butter. Bake pudding in middle of oven 50 minutes, or until set and top is crisp and golden brown.

Serve bread pudding warm or at room temperature with frozen yogurt.

Serves 6.

This charming menu pampers your guests with old-fashioned goodness. Delicate-tasting capon (a large young male chicken with plenty of tender white meat) is worth ordering fresh from your butcher. And, for dessert, two luscious pies ensure that everyone can try both. The cranberry pie has a furled lattice crust that looks fancy, but is easy to do. Simply twist the strips and arrange directly on the filling in lattice fashion, without weaving.

♦ Stock may be made 2 days ahead or frozen 1 month.

♦ Dressing may be made 2 days ahead.

♦ For the pies: Dough may be made 2 days ahead. (Make dough for each pie separately). Pies may be made 1 day ahead.

♦ Onions may be made 1 day ahead.

♦ Green beans may be made, in part, 1 day ahead.

TWO-PIE COUNTRY DINNER

ROAST CAPON WITH ROSEMARY CIDER GRAVY

---

*an 8- to 9-pound capon, thawed if frozen,
     reserving neck and giblets*
3 small apples, quartered
2 onions, quartered
2 tablespoons unsalted butter, softened
½ teaspoon dried thyme, crumbled
1 carrot, cut into 1-inch pieces
¾ cup apple cider
3 cups capon giblet stock (recipe follows)
4 tablespoons all-purpose flour
1 tablespoon dried rosemary, crumbled

Preheat oven to 425° F.

Rinse capon and pat dry inside and out. Season cavity with salt and pepper and put one third of apples and half of onions in cavity. With small metal or wooden skewers completely close body cavity and neck cavity and with kitchen string tie drumsticks together. Arrange capon, breast side up, in a roasting pan and rub all over with butter. Sprinkle capon with thyme and season with salt and pepper. Scatter remaining apples, remaining onion, and carrot in pan.

Roast capon in middle of oven 30 minutes. Reduce heat to 325° F. and baste capon with pan juices. Roast capon, basting every 15 minutes, 1 hour and 45 minutes more, or until juices run clear when fleshy part of a thigh is pierced with a skewer and a meat thermometer inserted in fleshy part of a thigh registers 180° F.

Remove string and skewers from capon and pour juices from inside capon into roasting pan. Transfer capon to a heated platter and let stand, covered loosely, 20 minutes.

Make gravy:

Transfer contents of roasting pan to a saucepan and skim off fat. To roasting pan add cider and on top of stove deglaze over moderately high heat, scraping up brown bits. Boil liquid in roasting pan until reduced by half and add to saucepan. In a small bowl whisk together ½ cup giblet stock and flour until smooth. To saucepan add remaining 2½ cups giblet stock and rosemary and boil 5 minutes. Add flour mixture in a stream, whisking, and simmer, whisking occasionally, 5 minutes. Season gravy with salt and pepper and pour through a sieve into a heated gravy boat.

Serve capon with gravy.

Serves 8.

CAPON GIBLET STOCK

---

*neck and giblets (excluding liver) from an
     8- to 9-pound capon*
8 cups water
1 celery rib, chopped
1 carrot, chopped
1 onion, quartered
1 apple, chopped
1 bay leaf
1 teaspoon whole black peppercorns

In a large saucepan bring all ingredients to a boil and cook, uncovered, at a bare simmer

2 hours, or until liquid is reduced to about 4 cups. Pour stock through a fine sieve into a 2-quart measuring cup (if more than 4 cups stock, simmer to reduce; if less, add water). *Stock may be made 2 days ahead and cooled completely, uncovered, before being chilled in airtight container, or frozen 1 month.*

Makes about 4 cups.

APPLE AND ANDOUILLE SAUSAGE DRESSING

¾ **pound andouille (Cajun) sausage or other spicy smoked sausage, sliced**
1 large onion, chopped
1 cup chopped celery
½ **stick (¼ cup) unsalted butter**
2 tart apples
a 16-ounce bag Pepperidge Farm seasoned bread stuffing (about 6 cups)
¼ **cup finely chopped fresh parsley leaves**
2 teaspoons fennel seeds
1½ **cups chicken broth**

Preheat oven to 350° F. and butter a 2½- to 3-quart baking dish.

In a large heavy skillet cook sausage, onion, and celery in butter over moderate heat, stirring, until onion is softened, about 20 minutes. Peel and core apples and chop. In a large bowl stir together sausage mixture, apples, and remaining ingredients with salt and pepper to taste and transfer to baking dish. *Dressing may be made 2 days ahead and chilled, covered.*

Bake dressing 30 minutes, or until heated through and top is golden.

Serves 8.

GREEN BEANS WITH WALNUTS

2 pounds green beans, trimmed and cut on the diagonal into 1½-inch pieces
2 tablespoons unsalted butter
2 large garlic cloves, minced
½ cup walnuts, chopped coarse

In a kettle of boiling salted water cook beans until barely tender, about 4 minutes. Drain beans and plunge into a bowl of ice water to stop cooking. Drain beans well and transfer to a bowl. *Beans may be prepared up to this point 1 day ahead and chilled, covered.*

In a large heavy skillet heat butter over moderate heat until foam subsides and cook garlic and walnuts, stirring, just until garlic begins to turn pale golden. Add beans and cook, stirring, until crisp-tender, about 3 minutes. Season beans with salt and pepper.

Serves 8.

GOLDEN SOUR CREAM ONIONS

2½ pounds small white onions (about 40) each 2 inches in diameter
2 tablespoons unsalted butter
1 teaspoon sugar
1 teaspoon caraway seeds
¾ teaspoon salt
½ cup sour cream

In a kettle of boiling water blanch onions in batches, 2 minutes, transferring to a colander to drain. When cool enough to handle, peel onions.

In a deep skillet just large enough to hold onions in one layer boil onions, butter, sugar, caraway seeds, salt, and enough water to cover onions by ½ inch until most of liquid is evaporated. Cook onions over moderate heat, swirling skillet, until golden and beginning to brown. Add sour cream and salt and pepper to taste and heat, stirring, until just heated through. *Onions may be made 1 day ahead and chilled, covered. Reheat onions in a skillet over moderately low heat, stirring, until hot.*

Serves 8.

CRANBERRY MAPLE PEAR PIE

—

1 pound firm-ripe pears

a 12-ounce bag fresh or frozen cranberries (about 3 cups), picked over

1 cup pure maple syrup

4½ teaspoons cornstarch dissolved in 2 tablespoons cold water

flaky pastry dough (recipe follows)

Peel and core firm-ripe pears and cut into ¼-inch pieces. In a saucepan bring cranberries, syrup, and pears to a boil and simmer, stirring occasionally, 3 minutes, or until cranberries have burst. Stir cornstarch mixture and stir into cranberry mixture. Simmer filling, stirring, 1 minute, or until thickened. Transfer filling to a bowl and cool. *Filling may be made 1 day ahead and chilled, covered.*

Preheat oven to 425° F.

On a lightly floured surface with a floured rolling pin roll out larger ball of dough into a ⅛-inch-thick round (about 12 inches in diameter). Fit dough into a 9-inch (1-quart capacity) pie plate and trim edge, leaving a ½-inch overhang. Chill scraps, wrapped in plastic wrap. Chill shell while cutting lattice.

Roll out other ball of dough ⅛ inch thick and with a fluted pastry wheel or a sharp knife cut into ½-inch-wide strips. On a baking sheet chill strips 10 minutes, or until just firm.

With tracing paper, trace maple leaf (right) and cut out a template from cardboard. On lightly floured surface roll out scraps ⅛ inch thick and on a small baking sheet freeze dough 5 minutes, or until just firm. Using template, cut out 2 leaves from dough with sharp knife and chill on baking sheet.

Spoon filling into shell, spreading evenly. Arrange half of pastry strips on top of filling about 1 inch apart, twisting each strip corkscrew fashion. Arrange remaining strips, twisting each strip, to form a lattice. Trim ends of strips flush with overhang of shell, pressing them onto shell. Turn up overhanging dough and crimp edge. Score pastry leaves decoratively with a knife and arrange on lattice.

Bake pie in upper third of oven 40 minutes, or until pastry is golden and filling is bubbling, and transfer to a rack to cool. *Pie may be made 1 day ahead and kept, covered loosely, at cool room temperature. Reheat pie in a preheated 350° F. oven 10 minutes, or until crust is crisp.* Serve pie warm or at room temperature.

Photo on page 42

FLAKY PASTRY DOUGH

—

2¼ *cups all-purpose flour*
½ *teaspoon salt*
½ *stick cold unsalted butter, cut into bits*
½ *cup cold vegetable shortening*
about 4 tablespoons ice water

In a bowl with a pastry blender blend flour, salt, and butter until mixture resembles coarse meal. Add shortening, cut into pieces, and blend until mixture resembles meal. Add ice water, 1 tablespoon at a time, tossing with a fork, until mixture forms a soft but not sticky dough and form into a ball. For a lattice pie, divide dough into 2 balls, one slightly larger than the other. *Dough may be made 2 days ahead and chilled, wrapped in plastic wrap.*

Makes enough pastry dough for a double-crust pie.

PECAN PUMPKIN PIE

—

½ *recipe flaky pastry dough (recipe above)*
FOR PUMPKIN MIXTURE
  ¾ *cup canned solid-pack pumpkin*
  2 *tablespoons packed light brown sugar*
  1 *large egg, beaten lightly*
  2 *tablespoons sour cream*
  ⅛ *teaspoon cinnamon*
  ⅛ *teaspoon freshly grated nutmeg*
FOR PECAN MIXTURE
  ¾ *cup light corn syrup*

½ *cup packed light brown sugar*
3 *large eggs, beaten lightly*
3 *tablespoons unsalted butter, melted and cooled*
2 *teaspoons vanilla*
¼ *teaspoon freshly grated lemon zest*
1½ *teaspoons fresh lemon juice*
¼ *teaspoon salt*
1⅓ *cups pecans*

Preheat oven to 425° F.

On a lightly floured surface with a floured rolling pin roll out dough into a 12-inch round. Fit dough into a 9-inch pie plate and crimp edge decoratively. Chill shell.

Make pumpkin mixture:

In a small bowl whisk together pumpkin mixture ingredients until smooth.

Make pecan mixture:

In a small bowl stir together all pecan mixture ingredients except pecans until combined well and stir in pecans.

Spread pumpkin mixture evenly in shell and spoon pecan mixture over it evenly, being careful not to disturb pumpkin layer.

Bake pie in upper third of oven 20 minutes. Reduce temperature to 350° F. and bake pie 20 minutes more, or until filling is slightly puffed. (Center will still tremble slightly.) Transfer pie to a rack to cool. *Pie may be made 4 hours ahead and kept, covered loosely, at cool room temperature or 1 day ahead and chilled, covered loosely. Reheat pie in a preheated 350° F. oven 10 minutes, or until crust is crisp.* Serve pie warm or at room temperature.

Photo on page 42

SPICED COCO-NUTS

LEMONGRASS TURKEY MEATBALLS

GINGER SCALLOPS WITH
STIR-FRIED BROCCOLI RABE

FRIED BASMATI RICE WITH
PINEAPPLE AND SCALLION

SESAME VEGETABLE SALAD

COCONUT CRÈME BRÛLÉE

Cloudy Bay Marlborough New Zealand
Sauvignon Blanc 1996

SERVES 8

Add some adventure to your life (and tastebuds) with this exotic East meets West menu. Food pairings such as coconuts with pecans, lemongrass with turkey, gingerroot with scallops, and basmati rice with pineapple introduce you to a palette of Asian flavors. Ideally, serve this menu as a buffet.

◆ Coco-nuts keep 2 weeks.

◆ Meatballs may be prepared 1 day ahead. Dipping sauce may be made 2 days ahead.

◆ Vegetable salad: vegetables and dressing may be prepared separately 1 day ahead.

◆ Custards for crème brûlée must be chilled at least 4 hours and up to 12.

◆ Scallops must marinate at least 1 hour and up to 12.

◆ Rice may be prepared, in part, 2 hours ahead.

PACIFIC RIM DINNER

SPICED COCO-NUTS

¹⁄₄ cup sugar

¹⁄₂ cup sweetened flaked coconut

2 teaspoons curry powder

¹⁄₈ teaspoon cayenne, or to taste

1 teaspoon salt

1 large egg white

*1 pound mixed nuts such as pecans, raw
     cashews, blanched almonds, and peanuts*

Preheat oven to 300° F. and butter a large
shallow baking pan.

In a large bowl stir together sugar,
coconut, curry powder, cayenne, and salt. In
another bowl whisk white until foamy and add
nuts, stirring until coated well. Add nuts to
coconut mixture, tossing until coated well,
and spread nuts in one layer in pan.

Roast nuts in middle of oven until pale
nuts are golden, 20 to 30 minutes. Cool nuts
completely in pan on a rack. (Nuts will crisp
as they cool.) *Nuts keep in an airtight container at room temperature 2 weeks.*

Makes about 4 cups.

LEMONGRASS TURKEY MEATBALLS

1 pound ground turkey

1 cup fine fresh bread crumbs

1 large egg, beaten lightly

*3 tablespoons minced tender inner part of
     lemongrass* (about 1 stalk)*

3 tablespoons minced fresh basil leaves

3 tablespoons minced fresh mint leaves

2 tablespoons grated onion

1 large garlic clove, minced

1¹⁄₂ teaspoons olive oil

¹⁄₂ teaspoon salt

vegetable oil for frying

ACCOMPANIMENT: **hot-and-sour dipping sauce
     (recipe follows)**

** available at Southeast Asian markets and by mail
     order (page 231)*

In a bowl stir together all ingredients except
vegetable oil until combined well and form
into 1¹⁄₄-inch meatballs, transferring to a tray.
*Meatballs may be prepared up to this point
1 day ahead and chilled, covered loosely.*

Preheat oven to 250° F.

In a large skillet heat ¹⁄₂ inch vegetable oil
over moderate heat until hot but not smoking
and fry meatballs in batches, shaking skillet
gently, 3 to 5 minutes, or until cooked through.
Transfer meatballs with a slotted spoon as
fried to paper towels to drain and keep warm,
covered, in oven up to 30 minutes.

Serve meatballs warm with dipping sauce.

Makes about 32 meatballs.

HOT-AND-SOUR DIPPING SAUCE

2 tablespoons bottled Chinese duck sauce*
1½ tablespoons fresh lime juice
1½ tablespoons Asian fish sauce*
2 tablespoons minced scallion
1 teaspoon minced fresh red chili
    (wear rubber gloves)

*available at Asian markets

In a small bowl whisk together all ingredients until combined well. *Sauce may be made 2 days ahead and chilled, covered.*

Makes about ½ cup.

GINGER SCALLOPS WITH STIR-FRIED BROCCOLI RABE

FOR SAUCE
    ¼ cup cornstarch
    ⅔ cup water
    ⅔ cup soy sauce
    ⅔ cup Chinese rice wine* or sake*
    ⅓ cup sugar
    3 tablespoons minced peeled fresh gingerroot
    1 teaspoon dried hot red pepper flakes

3 pounds sea scallops, tough muscles removed
2 bunches broccoli rabe (about 2 pounds)
sixteen 10-inch bamboo skewers, soaked in
    water to cover 1 hour

2 tablespoons vegetable oil
4 red bell peppers, cut into thin strips
⅔ cup water

* available at Asian markets

Make sauce:

In a saucepan stir cornstarch into water until dissolved and stir in remaining sauce ingredients. Bring mixture to a boil, whisking constantly, and simmer, whisking, 1 minute, or until slightly thickened. Cool sauce 5 minutes.

Transfer half of sauce to a bowl and reserve, covered and chilled. In another bowl toss scallops with remaining sauce. *Marinate scallops, covered and chilled, at least 1 hour and up to 12 hours.*

Remove coarse and hollow stems from broccoli rabe and discard. Cut stalks and leaves diagonally into 1½-inch pieces.

Prepare grill.

Thread scallops lengthwise onto skewers, discarding sauce used as marinade, and grill on an oiled rack set 5 to 6 inches over glowing coals 3 to 4 minutes on each side, or until just cooked through.

Heat a wok or deep 12-inch skillet over high heat until hot and add oil. Heat oil until it begins to smoke and stir-fry bell peppers 1 minute. Add broccoli rabe and stir-fry until slightly wilted and bright green, about 1 minute. Add water and cook, tightly covered, until greens are tender, 2 to 3 minutes. Add reserved sauce and cook, stirring, until vegetables are well coated and sauce is thickened.

Serve vegetables topped with scallops.

Serves 8.

Photo on page 50

FRIED BASMATI RICE WITH PINEAPPLE AND SCALLION

—

2 cups basmati rice*

2⅔ cups water

¾ teaspoon salt

1 cup chopped scallions

2 tablespoons vegetable oil

1 cup ¼-inch dice pineapple
(preferably fresh)

*available at specialty foods shops
and many supermarkets*

In a large bowl wash rice in several changes of cold water until water is clear. Cover rice with cold water by 3 inches and soak 30 minutes. Drain rice well.

In a large heavy saucepan bring rice, 2⅔ cups water, and salt to a boil and cook, covered, over low heat 15 minutes, or until tender and liquid is absorbed. Fluff rice with a fork. *Rice may be prepared up to this point 2 hours ahead and kept, uncovered, at room temperature.*

In a large non-stick skillet sauté scallion in oil, stirring, over moderately high heat 1 minute. Add rice and sauté, stirring, 5 minutes. Stir in pineapple and salt and pepper to taste and cook 1 minute, or until heated through.

Serves 8.

SESAME VEGETABLE SALAD

—

FOR VEGETABLES

2 cups julienne strips of peeled carrot

2 cups julienne strips of peeled seeded cucumber

2 cups julienne strips of peeled daikon (Japanese radish, about 1 pound)

1 cup bean sprouts, rinsed and drained well

3 scallions, sliced thin

¼ cup minced fresh coriander sprigs

FOR DRESSING

3 tablespoons rice vinegar (not seasoned)

1 tablespoon soy sauce

1 tablespoon honey

1 teaspoon anise seeds, crushed lightly

¼ cup vegetable oil

1 tablespoon Asian sesame oil

GARNISH: *1½ tablespoons toasted sesame seeds*

Make vegetables:

In a large bowl toss together vegetables and coriander. *Vegetables may be prepared 1 day ahead and chilled, covered.*

Make dressing:

In a small bowl whisk together vinegar, soy sauce, honey, anise seeds, and salt and pepper to taste and add oils in a stream, whisking until emulsified. *Dressing may be made 1 day ahead and chilled, covered.*

Toss salad with dressing and garnish with sesame seeds.

Serves 8.

COCONUT CRÈME BRÛLÉE

1¾ cups heavy cream

1¾ cups milk

1 vanilla bean, split lengthwise

6 large egg yolks

1 whole large egg

½ cup granulated sugar

⅔ cup packed sweetened flaked coconut,
  toasted golden, cooled, and crumbled
  coarse

¼ cup packed light brown sugar for broiling
  or raw sugar* if using a blowtorch

* available at natural foods stores
  and specialty foods shops

Preheat oven to 325° F.

In a heavy saucepan heat cream, milk, and vanilla bean until mixture just comes to a boil and remove pan from heat. Let mixture stand 10 minutes and with a knife scrape vanilla seeds into milk mixture, reserving pod for another use. In a bowl whisk together yolks, whole egg, and granulated sugar until combined well and add milk mixture in a stream, whisking. Skim any froth.

Divide coconut and custard among eight ½-cup flameproof ramekins set in a roasting pan and add enough hot water to pan to reach halfway up sides of ramekins.

Bake custards in middle of oven 40 minutes, or until they are just set but still tremble slightly. Remove ramekins from pan and cool custards. *Chill custards, loosely covered with plastic wrap, at least 4 hours and up to 12.*

Just before serving, set broiler rack so that custards will be 2 to 3 inches from heat and preheat broiler.

Sift brown sugar evenly over custards and broil custards until sugar is melted and caramelized, about 2 minutes. (Alternatively, raw sugar may be sprinkled over custards and caramelized with a blowtorch.)

Serves 8.

Photo above

PROSCIUTTO-WRAPPED ASPARAGUS

Alois Lageder Pinot Bianco
Alto Adige 1995

MUSHROOM CONSOMMÉ

ROAST PRIME RIB WITH HERBED HORSERADISH CRUST

POLENTA AND RED PEPPER HASH

SAUTÉED ESCAROLE WITH GARLIC

Caparzo La Caduta
Rosso di Montalcino 1992

CHOCOLATE GRAPPA CAKE

HONEY-GRAPPA COMPOTE

Grappa dei Barbi

SERVES 8

Although Italian in spirit, our holiday menu includes plenty of surprises—like star anise and horseradish. Our "hash" calls for store-bought polenta, which has the ideal firm texture for our recipe and can save you a step. Grappa, the fiery Italian brandy, ranges in quality and price. Our selection is delicious for sipping with our cake and compote.

♦ Consommé may be made 3 days ahead.

♦ Grappa cake may be made 2 days ahead.

♦ Asparagus hors d'oeuvres may be made 1 day ahead.

♦ Hash may be made 1 day ahead.

♦ Compote must be chilled at least 1 hour and up to 4.

A SPIRITED HOLIDAY DINNER

PROSCIUTTO-WRAPPED ASPARAGUS

30 medium-thin asparagus stalks (about
    1½ pounds)

4 ounces peppered Boursin cheese, softened

¼ pound thinly sliced prosciutto

¼ cup honey mustard

Trim asparagus so that spears are 5 inches long. In a deep skillet bring 1½ inches salted water to a boil and cook asparagus until crisp-tender, about 2 minutes. In a colander drain asparagus and rinse under cold water. Drain asparagus well on paper towels.

In a bowl mash Boursin with a fork until smooth. Cut 1 slice prosciutto lengthwise into 1-inch-wide strips and spread a strip with about ½ teaspoon Boursin. Spread about ¼ teaspoon mustard over Boursin and wrap prosciutto strip in a spiral around 1 asparagus spear, trimming any excess. Make more hors d'oeuvres with remaining prosciutto, Boursin, mustard, and asparagus in same manner. *Hors d'oeuvres may be made 1 day ahead and chilled, covered.*

Makes 30 hors d'oeuvres.

Photo on front jacket

MUSHROOM CONSOMMÉ

4 pounds fresh white mushrooms

1½ ounces dried morels*

2 cups chopped onion

1 cup chopped celery

1 whole star anise

1 tablespoon salt

3½ quarts water

2 tablespoons fresh lemon juice, or to taste

1 tablespoon Pernod or other anise-flavored
    liqueur, or to taste

GARNISH: *fine julienne strips of scallion greens*

* available at specialty foods shops and by mail order
    (page 231)

In a food processor or with a knife mince fresh mushrooms. In a kettle bring fresh mushrooms, dried morels, onion, celery, star anise, salt, and water to a boil, uncovered, and simmer 2 hours. Add lemon juice and pour consommé through a sieve lined with a double thickness of rinsed and squeezed cheesecloth into a large bowl, reserving morels. Stir in Pernod and salt and pepper to taste. *Consommé may be made 3 days ahead and cooled completely before being chilled, covered. Keep reserved morels, covered and chilled, separately. Reheat consommé before serving (do not boil).*

Serve consommé in heated soup bowls and garnish with scallion and reserved morels, halved if large.

Makes about 8 cups, serving 8.

ROAST PRIME RIB WITH HERBED HORSERADISH CRUST

a 4-rib standing rib roast (about 8 pounds trimmed)

FOR CRUST MIXTURE

    3 tablespoons drained bottled horseradish

    1 tablespoon Dijon mustard

    1 teaspoon coarsely ground black pepper

    1 teaspoon salt

    1 teaspoon dried thyme, crumbled

    1 teaspoon dried rosemary, crumbled

FOR SAUCE

    ⅔ cup dry red wine

    2 cups low-salt beef broth

    GARNISH: *fresh rosemary sprigs*

Let rib roast stand at room temperature 1 hour. Preheat oven to 450° F.

Make crust mixture:

In a small bowl stir together crust mixture ingredients until combined well.

In a flameproof roasting pan arrange rib roast, rib side down, and rub fat side with crust mixture. Roast beef in middle of oven 25 minutes. Reduce temperature to 300° F. and roast beef 2¾ hours more, or until a meat thermometer inserted in fleshy part registers 135° F. for medium-rare.

Transfer beef to a board and discard strings if necessary. Let beef stand, loosely covered, at least 20 minutes and up to 30 minutes before carving.

Make sauce while beef is standing:

Skim fat from drippings in roasting pan. Add wine and deglaze pan over moderately high heat, scraping up brown bits. Boil mixture until reduced by about half and transfer to a saucepan. Add broth and boil 5 minutes. Season sauce with salt and pepper.

Garnish rib roast with rosemary sprigs and serve with sauce.

Serves 8.

POLENTA AND RED PEPPER HASH

—

4 tablespoons olive oil plus additional
 tablespoon if necessary

a 24-ounce store-bought plain polenta roll*,
 cut into ½-inch cubes

1 large onion, cut into ¾-inch pieces
 (about 2 cups)

3 large garlic cloves, minced

3 red bell peppers, cut into ¾-inch squares
 (about 2 cups)

two 6-ounce jars marinated artichoke hearts,
 drained and chopped coarse (about 1½
 cups)

1¼ cups coarsely chopped pitted green olives

1 teaspoon dried oregano, crumbled

½ cup chopped fresh parsley leaves

1 tablespoon balsamic vinegar

¾ cup freshly grated Parmesan

*available at Italian markets, some supermarkets, and
 by mail order (page 231)

In a large non-stick skillet heat 2 tablespoons
oil over moderately high heat until hot but not
smoking and sauté half of polenta, stirring,
until golden, about 3 minutes. Transfer sautéed
polenta with a slotted spoon to a bowl. Sauté
remaining polenta in remaining 2 tablespoons
oil in same manner, transferring to bowl.

Add onion and garlic to skillet with additional oil if necessary and cook over moderate
heat, stirring, until onion is golden. Add bell
peppers, artichokes, olives, and oregano and
cook, stirring, 10 minutes. Add polenta,
parsley, vinegar, and salt and pepper to taste

and cook until heated through. *Hash may be
made up to this point 1 day ahead and cooled
completely before being chilled, covered. Reheat
hash in non-stick skillet over moderate heat.*
 Serve hash sprinkled with Parmesan.

Serves 8.

SAUTÉED ESCAROLE WITH GARLIC

 —

¼ cup plus 2 tablespoons extra-virgin olive oil

3 pounds escarole (about 3 large heads), cut
 into bite-size pieces

3 garlic cloves, sliced thin

In a 2-quart heavy kettle heat ¼ cup oil over
moderately high heat until hot but not smoking
and sauté one fourth escarole and one fourth
garlic, tossing with tongs, until escarole is
wilted slightly. Continue adding remaining
escarole and garlic, one fourth of each at a
time, and sautéing in same manner, until all
escarole is wilted and garlic is softened. Season
escarole mixture with salt and pepper and
transfer with tongs to a heated bowl. Boil
liquid remaining in kettle until reduced to
about 3 tablespoons. Drizzle escarole mixture
with reduced liquid and remaining 2 tablespoons oil and toss to coat well.

Serves 8.

CHOCOLATE GRAPPA CAKE

===

½ cup raisins

¾ cup plus 1 tablespoon all-purpose flour

9 ounces bittersweet chocolate, chopped

1 stick unsalted butter, cut into pieces

6 large eggs, separated

½ cup granulated sugar

⅓ cup grappa (Italian brandy)

1 teaspoon vanilla

⅓ cup pine nuts

GARNISH: *confectioners' sugar*

ACCOMPANIMENT: *whipped cream*

Preheat oven to 350° F. Butter a 9-inch springform pan and line bottom with a round of wax paper. Butter paper and dust pan with flour.

In a small bowl soak raisins in warm water to cover 20 minutes. Drain raisins and pat dry between paper towels. In a small bowl toss raisins with 1 tablespoon flour until coated.

In a metal bowl set over a saucepan of barely simmering water melt chocolate and butter, stirring occasionally, and remove bowl from heat. Cool mixture 5 minutes. In a large bowl whisk together yolks, sugar, grappa, and vanilla and add chocolate mixture, a spoonful at a time, stirring well after each addition. Add remaining ¾ cup flour, stirring until batter is just combined, and fold in raisins and pine nuts.

In another large bowl with an electric mixer beat whites with a pinch salt until they just hold soft peaks. Stir one fourth whites into batter to lighten and fold in remaining whites gently but thoroughly. Turn batter into springform pan and smooth top.

Bake cake in middle of oven 40 to 50 minutes, or until puffed and small cracks appear on top (center will be slightly moist). Cool cake in pan on a rack 10 minutes. Remove side and bottom of pan and wax paper and cool cake completely on rack.

Dust cake lightly with confectioners' sugar and serve with whipped cream.

Photo on page 56

HONEY-GRAPPA COMPOTE

===

⅓ cup honey

⅓ cup grappa (Italian brandy)

1 tablespoon fresh lemon juice

2 pink grapefruits

2 navel oranges

1 pint strawberries, hulled and sliced

1 cup halved seedless green grapes

In a large bowl whisk together honey, grappa, and lemon juice. With a sharp knife cut away peel and pith from grapefruits and oranges. Working over bowl, cut sections free from membranes, letting sections drop into bowl, and squeeze membranes for juice. Add strawberries and grapes and toss gently. *Chill compote, covered, at least 1 hour and up to 4.*

Serves 8.

Photo on page 56

Sophisticated and always in style, a fancy cocktail party is a lovely way to entertain a large group. Ours even includes two little desserts, so most guests will happily make a meal of this generous menu.

Each hors d'oeuvre can be made, in part, ahead of time. Then, on the day of your party:

◆ 3 hours ahead: Arrange desserts on trays and chill.

◆ 2 hours ahead: Pan-fry Sesame Chicken (reheat just before serving). Then, assemble: Walnut Salad in Endive, Southwestern Beef Canapés, and Curried Scallop Canapés on separate platters.

◆ 45 minutes ahead: Bake Brie en Croûte and Worcestershire Mushroom Rolls and serve warm.

CURRIED SCALLOP CANAPÉS

WALNUT SALAD IN ENDIVE

WORCESTERSHIRE MUSHROOM ROLLS

BRIE BAKED EN CROÛTE WITH TOMATO CHUTNEY

SESAME CHICKEN

SOUTHWESTERN BEEF CANAPÉS

CITRUS COCONUT TRIANGLES

TOFFEE BOURBON TRUFFLES

Martinis

Langtry Guenoc Valley White Meritage 1995

Roederer Estate Anderson Valley Brut

SERVES 18 TO 24

AN ELEGANT COCKTAIL PARTY

Curried Scallop Canapés

1 teaspoon curry powder

1 cup canned unsweetened coconut milk*, stirred well

¼ cup fresh lime juice, or to taste

½ teaspoon salt, or to taste

½ pound bay or sea scallops

2 Asian pears*

8 to 10 kumquats*

about 40 fresh coriander leaves

* available at Asian markets and some specialty foods shops and supermarkets

In a 1-quart heavy saucepan stir curry powder into about 1 tablespoon coconut milk until dissolved. Stir in 1 teaspoon lime juice, salt, and remaining coconut milk and simmer over moderately low heat 10 minutes, or until thickened.

Remove tough muscle from side of each scallop if necessary. If using sea scallops, cut into ½-inch pieces. Add scallops to coconut milk mixture and poach at a bare simmer until just cooked through but still tender, 2 to 3 minutes. Transfer scallops with poaching liquid to a small bowl and cool. *Scallops may be poached 1 day ahead and chilled, covered.*

Core Asian pears and cut crosswise into ¼-inch-thick rounds. Cut rounds into 1-inch wedges and in a small bowl toss with remaining lime juice. *Macerate pears, covered and chilled, at least 15 minutes and up to 3 hours.*

Just before serving, cut kumquats crosswise into thin rounds. Arrange pear wedges, drained, on platter and top each with 1

kumquat slice, 1 coriander leaf, and 1 piece of scallop coated with poaching liquid.

Makes about 40 canapés.

Photo opposite and on page 62

Walnut Salad in Endive

1 small garlic clove, minced and mashed to a paste with ½ teaspoon salt

2 tablespoons fresh lemon juice

2 tablespoons extra-virgin olive oil

1 tablespoon mayonnaise

a ¼-pound piece of Parmesan, sliced ⅛ inch thick and cut into ⅛-inch dice (about 1 cup)

½ cup finely chopped celery

4 Belgian endives

1 cup walnuts, toasted lightly and chopped fine

¼ cup finely chopped fresh flat-leafed parsley leaves

In a bowl whisk together garlic paste, lemon juice, oil, and mayonnaise and stir in Parmesan and celery. *Salad may be prepared up to this point 1 day ahead and chilled, covered.*

Trim endives and separate leaves. *Endive leaves may be prepared up to this point 1 day ahead and chilled, wrapped in dampened paper towels, in a plastic bag.*

Stir walnuts and parsley into salad. Spoon about 1 tablespoon salad onto wide end of each endive leaf.

Makes about 40 hors d'oeuvres.

Photo opposite and on page 62

WORCESTERSHIRE
MUSHROOM ROLLS

———

¾ pound mushrooms, quartered
¼ pound shallots (about 3), minced
5 tablespoons unsalted butter
¼ cup Worcestershire sauce
¼ cup grated Cheddar
14 very thin slices firm white sandwich bread

GARNISH: *28 long fresh chives*

In a food processor mince mushrooms in 2 batches. In a 10-inch non-stick skillet cook shallots in 2 tablespoons butter over moderate heat, stirring, until golden. Add mushrooms with salt to taste and cook over moderate heat, stirring occasionally, until dark brown and very dry, about 15 minutes. Add Worcestershire sauce and simmer, stirring occasionally, until sauce is evaporated and mixture is very dry, about 5 minutes. Remove skillet from heat and stir in Cheddar. *Filling may be made 3 days ahead and chilled, covered.*

Discard crusts from bread and with a rolling pin flatten each slice into a larger rectangle. In a small saucepan melt remaining 3 tablespoons butter. On a work surface arrange a bread slice with a long side facing you and mound a level tablespoon filling along long side. Roll up bread jelly-roll fashion. Put roll, seam side down, in a shallow baking pan. Make more rolls with remaining bread and filling in same manner, arranging in pan in one layer, touching each other, and keeping covered with plastic wrap. Brush rolls all over with melted butter and rearrange, seam sides down and barely touching, in pan. *Chill mushroom rolls, covered, at least 1 hour and up to 1 day.*

Preheat oven to 425° F.

Bake mushroom rolls in upper third of oven 15 minutes, or until golden. Halve rolls crosswise and tie a chive around each half.

Makes 28 hors d'oeuvres.

Photo on page 62

Brie Baked en Croûte with Tomato Chutney

===

a 17¼-ounce package frozen puff pastry sheets, thawed

a 1-pound wheel Brie, chilled

about 2½ cups tomato chutney (recipe follows) or bottled tomato chutney

1 large egg, beaten lightly

ACCOMPANIMENT: *crusty bread or crackers*

On a lightly floured surface roll out 1 pastry sheet ⅛ inch thick (about 15 inches in diameter) and, using Brie as a guide, cut out 1 round the size of Brie. With a 2¾-inch star-shaped cutter cut out 5 stars from trimmings. Reserve pastry round and stars.

Halve Brie horizontally. Roll out remaining pastry sheet ⅛ inch thick (about 15 inches in diameter) and transfer to a shallow baking pan, about 15½ by 10½ inches. Center bottom half of Brie, cut side up, on pastry in pan and spread ½ cup tomato chutney onto Brie, leaving a ½-inch border. Top chutney with remaining half of Brie, cut side down.

Without stretching pastry, wrap up over Brie and trim excess to leave a 1-inch border on top of Brie. Brush border with some egg and top with reserved pastry round, pressing edges of dough together gently but firmly to seal. Brush top of pastry with some egg and arrange reserved stars decoratively on it. Lightly brush stars with some egg, being careful not to let egg drip over edges of stars (which would prevent them from rising). With back of a table knife gently score side of pastry with vertical marks (do not pierce dough). Chill Brie, uncovered, 30 minutes to set egg wash. *Brie may be prepared up to this point 1 day ahead and chilled, covered loosely.*

Preheat oven to 425° F.

Bake Brie in middle of oven 20 minutes, or until crust is puffed and golden. Let Brie stand in pan on a rack about 20 minutes for very runny melted cheese or about 40 minutes for thicker melted cheese and serve with remaining tomato chutney and bread or crackers.

Serves 18 to 24 as an hors d'oeuvre.

Photo below

TOMATO CHUTNEY

===

a 28- to 32-ounce can whole tomatoes,
    chopped, including juice

1 large onion, chopped (about 1 cup)

zest of 1 lemon, removed with a vegetable
    peeler and minced

$^1/_2$ cup sugar

$^1/_2$ cup cider vinegar

$^1/_3$ cup dried currants

1$^1/_2$ teaspoons mustard seeds

$^1/_2$ teaspoon salt

$^1/_4$ teaspoon cayenne

$^1/_4$ teaspoon ground allspice

$^1/_4$ teaspoon cinnamon

In a heavy kettle stir together all ingredients
and cook over moderate heat, stirring occasionally, 30 minutes. Reduce heat to low and
simmer mixture, stirring occasionally, 30 minutes more, or until thickened and reduced to
about 2$^1/_2$ cups. *Chutney keeps, covered and
chilled, 3 months.*

Makes about 2$^1/_2$ cups.

SESAME CHICKEN

===

For dipping sauce

1$^1/_2$ tablespoons dry mustard stirred together
    with 1$^1/_2$ tablespoons hot water

1$^1/_2$ cups mayonnaise

1 tablespoon fresh lemon juice, or to taste

3 tablespoons honey

3 tablespoons minced fresh chives or
    scallion greens

4 pounds skinless boneless chicken breasts,
    cut into 1-inch pieces

2 teaspoons Asian sesame oil

1 tablespoon minced garlic

2 large eggs, beaten lightly

1$^1/_2$ cups sesame seeds (about 6 ounces)

2 cups fresh bread crumbs

1 teaspoon salt

vegetable oil for frying

Make sauce:

In a small bowl whisk together sauce
ingredients until combined well. *Sauce may
be made 1 day ahead and chilled, covered.*

Line 3 trays with wax paper. In a bowl
toss chicken with sesame oil and garlic and
add eggs, tossing to coat chicken. In another
bowl stir together sesame seeds, fresh bread
crumbs, salt, and pepper to taste. Remove
chicken pieces, 1 at a time, from bowl, letting
excess egg drip off, and coat with sesame seed
mixture, transferring to trays. *Chicken may be
prepared up to this point 1 day ahead and
chilled, covered with plastic wrap.*

Preheat oven to 250° F.

In each of 2 large skillets heat $^1/_4$ inch
vegetable oil over moderate heat until hot but
not smoking and fry chicken in batches 2
minutes on each side, or until coating is crisp
and browned, transferring to paper towels to
drain. Keep chicken warm on baking sheets in
oven up to 30 minutes. *Alternatively, cooked
chicken may be kept at room temperature up to
2 hours and reheated in batches in a 300° F.
oven until hot.*

Serve chicken with sauce for dipping.

*Makes about 150 hors d'oeuvres,
serving 24.*

SOUTHWESTERN BEEF CANAPÉS

FOR POTATO ROUNDS

> *2 large long narrow sweet potatoes (about 1½ pounds), left unpeeled and scrubbed*
>
> *2 tablespoons vegetable oil*
>
> *coarse salt for sprinkling potatoes*

FOR BEEF MIXTURE

> *½ pound thinly sliced rare roast beef*
>
> *a 15-ounce can black beans, rinsed and drained*
>
> *1 red or yellow bell pepper, chopped fine*
>
> *¼ cup thinly sliced scallion*
>
> *2 tablespoons vegetable oil*
>
> *1 tablespoon fresh lime juice*

FOR CHIPOTLE SAUCE

> *2 teaspoons minced canned chipotle chili in adobo sauce**
>
> *¼ cup sour cream*
>
> *¼ cup mayonnaise*
>
> ** available at Latino markets and by mail order (page 231)*

Make potato rounds:

Preheat oven to 450° F. and oil 2 baking sheets.

Cut sweet potatoes crosswise into about seventy-five ⅛-inch-thick rounds. Arrange rounds in one layer on baking sheets (make sure rounds do not touch) and brush with oil. Roast rounds in batches in upper third of oven 9 minutes on each side, or until golden and slightly crisp. Transfer rounds as roasted to paper towels to drain and sprinkle with coarse salt and pepper to taste. *Potato rounds may be made 1 day ahead and cooled completely before being chilled, covered. Reheat rounds in a 350° F. oven until heated through before assembling hors d'oeuvres.*

Make beef mixture:

Cut roast beef into fine julienne strips and in a bowl toss with remaining beef mixture ingredients and salt to taste until combined well. *Beef mixture may be made 1 day ahead and chilled, covered.*

Make chipotle sauce:

In a bowl stir together sauce ingredients until combined well. *Sauce may be made 1 day ahead and chilled, covered.*

Mound about 1 tablespoon beef mixture on each sweet potato round and top with a dollop of sauce.

Makes about 75 hors d'oeuvres.

CITRUS COCONUT TRIANGLES

2¹/₂ cups all-purpose flour

*2¹/₂ sticks (1¹/₄ cups) cold unsalted butter,
    cut into bits*

²/₃ cup confectioners' sugar

5 large eggs, beaten lightly

2 cups granulated sugar

*1¹/₂ tablespoons freshly grated tangerine or
    orange zest*

¹/₃ cup fresh tangerine or orange juice

3 tablespoons fresh lemon juice

*1 cup sweetened flaked coconut, toasted
    lightly*

1¹/₄ teaspoons baking powder

GARNISH: *confectioners' sugar*

Preheat oven to 350° F. and butter a 15¹/₂- by
10¹/₂-inch jelly-roll pan.

In a bowl with a pastry blender or 2 knives
blend together flour, butter, and confectioners'
sugar until mixture resembles meal and pat
evenly into pan. Bake crust in middle of oven
15 to 18 minutes, or until pale golden.

In a large bowl stir together remaining
ingredients until combined well and pour over
crust. Bake dessert in middle of oven 20 to 25
minutes, or until golden and set. Cool dessert
completely in pan on a rack. *Chill dessert,
loosely covered, at least 1 hour and up to 3 days.*

Sift confectioners' sugar over dessert. Cut
dessert into 2-inch squares and cut squares
diagonally in half.

Makes about 70 triangles.

TOFFEE BOURBON TRUFFLES

¹/₂ cup heavy cream

*12 ounces fine-quality bittersweet chocolate
    (not unsweetened), chopped fine*

*¹/₂ stick (¹/₄ cup) unsalted butter, cut into bits
    and softened*

1 cup toffee bits or brickle bits

2 tablespoons bourbon

*about ¹/₂ cup unsweetened cocoa powder,
    sifted, for coating truffles*

In a saucepan bring cream just to a boil over
moderate heat and remove pan from heat.
Add chocolate, stirring until melted. Cool
mixture slightly. Add butter, bit by bit, stirring
until smooth. Stir in toffee or brickle bits,
bourbon, and a pinch salt and transfer to a
bowl. *Chill truffle mixture, covered, 4 hours, or
until firm.*

Line a baking sheet with wax paper. Form
mixture by heaping teaspoons into balls and
roll in cocoa powder. *Chill truffles on baking
sheet 1 hour, or until firm. Truffles keep in an
airtight container, chilled, 2 weeks.*

Makes about 40 truffles.

2

KITCHEN PARTIES

BUTTERNUT SQUASH RISOTTO

FENNEL, BIBB LETTUCE, AND
RADICCHIO SALAD

PEAR CRANBERRY CLAFOUTI

Bolla Valpolicella 1995

SERVES 4

W

here better to savor old-world dishes like risotto and clafouti than in your kitchen on a chilly evening with friends? Risotto, a northern Italian "creamy" rice entrée, requires your undivided attention and must be served as soon as it is ready. We've added butternut squash to our recipe for buttery flavor; to save on preparation time, bake the squash the day before. The only accompaniment you'll need is a simple salad—ours includes uncooked sliced fennel for sweet anise flavor and crunch. The clafouti, a French custardy fruit pudding normally made with cherries or dried prunes, has been varied with pears and cranberries. It is delicious when served warm, so ask a friend to finish stirring the risotto while you assemble the clafouti. If you put it in the oven as you sit down to dinner, it will be ready when you are.

◆ Butternut squash for the risotto may be prepared 1 day ahead.

A WARMING
RUSTIC SUPPER

BUTTERNUT SQUASH RISOTTO

==

1 large butternut squash (about 3 pounds)

3½ cups chicken broth

1 cup water

1 large onion, chopped (about 1¾ cups)

2 large garlic cloves, sliced thin

2½ teaspoons minced peeled fresh gingerroot

5 tablespoons unsalted butter

1 cup Arborio or long-grain rice

½ cup dry white wine

¼ cup chopped fresh chives

GARNISH: *chopped fresh chives and Parmesan curls shaved with a vegetable peeler from a ¼-pound piece of Parmesan at room temperature*

Preheat oven to 450° F. and generously oil a large shallow baking pan.

Halve squash lengthwise and discard seeds. Put 1 half, cut side down, in pan and bake in middle of oven 15 minutes. Peel remaining half and cut into ¼-inch dice. Add diced squash to pan, spreading in one layer, and season with salt and pepper. Bake squash in middle of oven, stirring diced squash occasionally, 15 minutes, or until all squash is tender. Scoop out flesh of squash half, holding it in a kitchen towel, and chop coarse. *Squash may be prepared 1 day ahead and cooled completely, uncovered, before being chilled, covered.*

In a saucepan bring broth and water to a simmer and keep at a bare simmer.

In a heavy kettle (about 4 quarts) cook onion, garlic, and gingerroot in butter over moderately low heat, stirring, until softened. Stir in rice and cook over moderate heat, stirring constantly, 1 minute. Add wine and cook, stirring, until absorbed. Stir in ¼ cup broth and cook, stirring constantly and keeping at a simmer throughout, until absorbed. Continue simmering and adding broth, about ¼ cup at a time, stirring constantly and letting each addition be absorbed before adding next, until about half of broth has been added. Stir in diced and chopped squash and continue simmering and adding broth in same manner until rice is tender and creamy-looking but still *al dente*, about 20 minutes. Stir in chives and salt and pepper to taste.

Serve risotto garnished with chives and Parmesan curls.

Serves 4.

Photo on page 72

FENNEL, BIBB LETTUCE, AND RADICCHIO SALAD

1 small fennel bulb (sometimes called anise), stalks trimmed flush with bulb
1½ cups torn radicchio leaves
2 cups torn Bibb lettuce
¼ cup Kalamata or other brine-cured black olives, pitted and sliced
1 tablespoon red-wine vinegar
¼ cup extra-virgin olive oil

Quarter fennel and cut away core, discarding it. With a sharp knife cut fennel lengthwise into very thin slices. Arrange *radicchio* and Bibb lettuce leaves on 4 plates and top with fennel and olives. In a small bowl whisk together vinegar and salt and pepper to taste and whisk in oil in a stream until emulsified. Drizzle vinaigrette over salads.

Serves 4.

PEAR CRANBERRY CLAFOUTI

4 firm-ripe pears (about 1½ pounds)
⅔ cup picked-over cranberries
1¼ cups milk
½ stick (¼ cup) unsalted butter, melted and cooled
3 large eggs, beaten lightly
1 teaspoon vanilla
¾ cup all-purpose flour
½ cup plus 3 tablespoons sugar
¼ cup chopped walnuts
¼ teaspoon cinnamon

Preheat oven to 400° F. and butter a 10- by 2-inch round baking dish (1-quart capacity).

Peel and core pears and slice thin lengthwise. In baking dish toss together pears and cranberries and spread evenly.

In a blender blend milk, 2 tablespoons butter, eggs, vanilla, flour, and ½ cup sugar until smooth and pour batter over fruit. In a small bowl stir together remaining 3 tablespoons sugar, walnuts, and cinnamon. Sprinkle walnut mixture over *clafouti* and drizzle with remaining 2 tablespoons butter.

Bake *clafouti* in middle of oven 40 minutes, or until custard is set and pears are tender, and cool on a rack 15 minutes. Serve *clafouti* warm.

Serves 4 generously.

Simple yet impressive, this little dinner is filled with the sunny flavors of Provence—seafood, a splash of Pernod, plenty of garlic, and a medley of herbs—tarragon, thyme, and chives. It is essential that all ingredients be absolutely fresh. If you are able to find cultivated mussels, they are the best choice. Otherwise, avoid overly heavy wild mussels; they may be filled with sand and will ruin the stew if they open! If necessary, any firm white fish (such as halibut or cod) may substitute for the monkfish. For dessert, our lemony madeleines, a moist and intensely flavored version of the tea cakes that the French adore, are sublime.

◆ Madeleines may be made 2 days ahead.

◆ Seafood Stew: Mussels may be scrubbed and beards removed 2 hours ahead. Shrimp may be shelled and deveined 2 hours ahead.

A PROVENÇAL DINNER

Seafood Stew

===

3 large garlic cloves, minced

2½ cups chopped onions

⅓ cup vegetable oil

1 pound boiling potatoes

3 carrots, cut into ¼-inch-thick slices

2 cups bottled clam juice

a 28- to 32-ounce can whole tomatoes,
    chopped, including juice

1 cup dry white wine

1 large green bell pepper, cut into matchsticks

1 pound mussels (preferably cultivated),
    scrubbed well and beards pulled off

1½ pounds monkfish, cut into 1-inch pieces

½ pound medium shrimp (about 12),
    shelled and deveined

1 tablespoon fresh tarragon leaves,
    chopped fine, or 1 teaspoon dried
    tarragon, crumbled

2 tablespoons Pernod or other anise-flavored
    liqueur if desired

ACCOMPANIMENT: *garlic toasts (recipe follows)*

In a 4-quart kettle cook garlic and onions in oil over moderately low heat, stirring, until softened. Peel potatoes and cut into ½-inch cubes. To onion mixture add potatoes, carrots, clam juice, tomatoes and their juice, and wine. Bring mixture to a boil and simmer 40 minutes, or until carrots and potatoes are tender. Add bell pepper and mussels and simmer, covered, 2 minutes, or until mussels begin to open. Add monkfish, shrimp, tarragon, and salt and pepper to taste and simmer, covered, 5 minutes, or until fish is cooked through. Discard any unopened mussels and stir in Pernod.

Serve stew with toasts.

Serves 4.

Photo on page 76

Garlic Toasts

 ===

¼ cup mayonnaise

2 teaspoons minced fresh chives

1 teaspoon paprika

a pinch cayenne, or to taste

1 teaspoon fresh lemon juice

four ½- to ¾-inch-thick bread slices cut from
    a 9-inch round of crusty bread

2 garlic cloves, halved lengthwise

Preheat broiler.

In a small bowl whisk together mayonnaise, chives, paprika, cayenne, and lemon juice.

Toast bread on a rack under broiler about 4 inches from heat, turning once, until pale golden. Rub one side of each toast with garlic and spread with mayonnaise mixture. Broil toasts 30 seconds more, or until top is just golden. Cut toasts into 1½-inch-wide strips.

Serves 4.

Lemon Thyme Madeleines with Lemon Vodka Syrup

═══

FOR MADELEINES

   2 cups cake flour (not self-rising)

   1 teaspoon baking powder

   ½ teaspoon salt

   3 tablespoons plus 1 teaspoon freshly grated
      lemon zest (from about 7 large lemons)

   1½ tablespoons finely chopped fresh
      thyme leaves

   2 sticks (1 cup) unsalted butter, softened

   2 teaspoons fresh lemon juice

   2 cups sugar

   6 large eggs

FOR LEMON SYRUP

   ¼ cup water

   ¼ cup sugar

   ¼ cup lemon vodka

   ¼ cup fresh lemon juice

   2 teaspoons finely chopped fresh thyme leaves

Make *madeleines*:

   Preheat oven to 325° F. and generously butter and flour *madeleine* molds (preferably non-stick), knocking out excess flour.

   In a bowl whisk together flour, baking powder, salt, zest, and thyme. In a large bowl with an electric mixer beat together butter, lemon juice, and sugar until light and fluffy. Add eggs, 1 at a time, beating well after each addition, and add flour mixture, beating until just combined.

   Fill *madeleine* molds with batter and with a spatula level tops, scraping back and forth over molds and returning excess batter to bowl. (This will eliminate any air pockets and ensure that molds are not overfilled.) Wipe excess batter from edges of pan.

   Bake *madeleines* in middle of oven 20 minutes, or until edges are browned and tops are golden. Loosen edges with a knife and transfer *madeleines* to a rack set over a baking sheet.

Make lemon syrup while *madeleines* are baking:

   In a small saucepan bring syrup ingredients to a boil, stirring, and remove pan from heat. Keep syrup warm.

   Brush warm *madeleines* with some warm syrup. Clean *madeleine* molds and butter and flour again. Make more *madeleines* with remaining batter and warm syrup in same manner. *Madeleines brushed with syrup may be made 2 days ahead. Cool madeleines completely before storing in an airtight container, layers separated by plastic wrap, at cool room temperature.*

   Makes about 42 madeleines.

SPAGHETTI WITH EGGPLANT
AND TOMATO SAUCE

BREADSTICKS (STORE-BOUGHT)

CAESAR SALAD

—

AMARETTO SOUFFLÉ CHEESECAKE

—

*Silverado Vineyards Napa Valley
Sangiovese 1994*

SERVES 4

You can never have enough exciting recipes for pasta, Caesar salad, and cheesecake—here is a menu that offers all three. Our simple eggplant and tomato sauce calls for canned tomatoes so it can be enjoyed year-round. Look for firm, shiny, unbruised eggplants, and pasta imported from Italy (De Cecco and Del Verde are two good brands). Our delicious Caesar salad can be composed in a large wooden bowl in minutes; and it's eggless, making it worry-free. Breadsticks—especially thin, crisp grissini—make an ideal accompaniment. You can put them out beforehand for snacking, too. As for our cheesecake, a dusting of ground Amaretti cookie crumbs act as a crust, making it extremely quick to prepare.

◆ Cheesecake must be chilled at least 4 hours and up to 1 day.

PASTA IN CUCINA SUPPER

Spaghetti with Eggplant and Tomato Sauce

—

1 pound spaghetti

2 pounds eggplant (about 2 medium)

6 tablespoons olive oil

1 onion, chopped

2 garlic cloves, minced

3 pounds canned whole tomatoes including juice

Preheat oven to 400° F. and bring a kettle of salted water to a boil for spaghetti.

Cut eggplant into ½-inch cubes. Divide eggplant between 2 shallow baking pans and drizzle with 4 tablespoons oil. Bake eggplant in upper and lower thirds of oven, stirring once and switching position of pans halfway through baking, 20 minutes, or until very tender and golden.

While eggplant is baking, in a large heavy saucepan cook onion and garlic in remaining 2 tablespoons oil over moderately low heat, stirring occasionally, until onion is softened. Add tomatoes with juice and simmer, uncovered, breaking up tomatoes and stirring occasionally, 15 minutes, or until thickened. Add eggplant to sauce and season with salt and pepper. Keep sauce warm.

Cook spaghetti in boiling water until *al dente* and drain well.

Serve spaghetti topped with sauce.

Serves 4.

Photo on page 80

Caesar Salad

1 large garlic clove, halved

3 tablespoons fresh lemon juice

1½ teaspoons Dijon mustard

1½ teaspoons Worcestershire sauce

3 flat anchovy fillets, minced

2 tablespoons mayonnaise

¼ cup extra-virgin olive oil

1 large or 2 small heads romaine, torn into pieces (about 12 cups)

3 tablespoons freshly grated Parmesan

Rub bottom of a large wooden salad bowl with garlic dipped in salt. Add lemon juice, mustard, Worcestershire sauce, anchovies, mayonnaise, and salt and pepper to taste and whisk until combined well. Add oil in a stream, whisking until emulsified. Add romaine and toss well. Sprinkle salad with Parmesan.

Serves 4.

AMARETTO SOUFFLÉ CHEESECAKE

═══

¼ cup finely ground amaretti*
  (Italian almond macaroons)
12 ounces cream cheese at room temperature
½ cup sugar
1 tablespoon all-purpose flour
3 large eggs, separated
¼ cup sour cream

3 tablespoons DiSaronno Amaretto
  (almond-flavored liqueur)
¼ teaspoon salt

* available at specialty foods shops and some
  supermarkets

Preheat oven to 350° F. Generously butter a 9-inch springform pan and add *amaretti* crumbs, shaking pan to coat bottom and sides.

In a bowl with an electric mixer beat together cream cheese, sugar, and flour until light and fluffy. Beat in yolks, sour cream, Amaretto, and salt until smooth. In another bowl beat whites until they just hold soft peaks. Fold one third of whites into cream cheese mixture to lighten and fold in remaining whites gently but thoroughly. Pour filling into pan.

Bake cheesecake in middle of oven 30 minutes, or until just set, and cool completely in pan on a rack. *Chill cheesecake, covered, at least 4 hours and up to 1 day.*

Since election night doesn't roll around that often, keep this cheerful all-American dinner in mind for Veterans Day, Presidents' Day, or any wintry gathering. Chicken potpie is a universal favorite, and ours is packed with extras like pearl onions, mushrooms, shallots, even piped potatoes. This, and the fact that it can be completely assembled a full day ahead, makes it an ideal company dish.

Likewise, the apple pie can be made the day before if you are willing to forego its wonderful aroma filling your kitchen on the night of your party. If you bake the pie ahead, warm it gently in your oven before serving.

◆ Chicken potpie may be assembled 1 day ahead.

◆ Apple pie may be made 1 day ahead. Pie dough must be chilled 1 hour before rolling out.

ELECTION NIGHT DINNER

CHICKEN POTPIE WITH CHIVE MASHED POTATOES

===

FOR FILLING

$2\frac{1}{2}$ quarts water

1 teaspoon salt

3 whole chicken breasts with skin and bones
   (about 3 pounds total)

$\frac{1}{2}$ pound small pearl onions (about 2 cups),
   left unpeeled and rinsed if necessary

1 pound mushrooms, quartered

$\frac{3}{4}$ stick (6 tablespoons) unsalted butter

3 medium carrots, cut into $\frac{1}{4}$-inch-
   thick slices

3 celery ribs, halved lengthwise and cut into
   $\frac{1}{4}$-inch-thick slices

$\frac{3}{4}$ cup thawed frozen peas

1 cup finely chopped shallots (about 4 large)

1 bay leaf

1 tablespoon fresh thyme leaves, chopped

$1\frac{1}{2}$ teaspoons dried tarragon, crumbled

$\frac{1}{3}$ cup all-purpose flour

$\frac{1}{4}$ cup plus 1 tablespoon medium-dry Sherry

freshly grated nutmeg to taste

FOR MASHED POTATOES

$2\frac{1}{2}$ pounds russet (baking) potatoes (about 5)

3 tablespoons unsalted butter, melted

1 cup sour cream

$\frac{1}{4}$ cup minced fresh chives

Make filling:

In a 5-quart saucepan bring $2\frac{1}{2}$ quarts water with salt to a boil. Add chicken and simmer, uncovered, 10 minutes. Add onions and simmer 10 minutes. Remove pan from heat and transfer onions with a slotted spoon to a bowl of ice water. Drain onions and cut off root ends. Peel onions. Let chicken stand in cooking liquid 30 minutes. With tongs transfer chicken to a large bowl and boil cooking liquid until reduced to about 1 quart stock. When chicken is cool enough to handle, discard skin and bones and cut meat into $\frac{3}{4}$-inch cubes. Return chicken to bowl.

In a large skillet cook mushrooms in 2 tablespoons butter over moderate heat, stirring, until golden brown and liquid they give off is evaporated and add to chicken. In skillet cook carrots, celery, and onions in 1 tablespoon butter over moderate heat, stirring, 5 minutes. Add 1 cup stock and salt and pepper to taste and simmer until vegetables are just tender. Boil mixture over high heat until liquid is evaporated and vegetables are glazed. Add glazed vegetables and peas to chicken mixture.

In skillet cook shallots with bay leaf, thyme, and tarragon in remaining 3 tablespoons butter over moderately low heat, stirring, until pale golden and stir in flour. Cook mixture, stirring, 3 minutes (it will look crumbly) and gradually whisk in remaining 3 cups stock, $\frac{1}{4}$ cup Sherry, nutmeg, and salt and pepper to taste. Simmer sauce, whisking occasionally, about 5 minutes and whisk in remaining tablespoon Sherry. Discard bay leaf and pour sauce over chicken mixture, stirring until combined well.

Preheat oven to 425° F.

Make potatoes:

Peel potatoes and cut into 1-inch pieces. In a saucepan cover potatoes with water by 1 inch and simmer until very tender, 10 to 15 minutes. Reserve about ½ cup cooking liquid and drain potatoes. Force potatoes in batches through a ricer or food mill fitted with medium disk into a bowl and stir in reserved cooking liquid, butter, sour cream, chives, and salt and pepper to taste. Transfer potatoes to a pastry bag fitted with a ½-inch fluted tip.

Spread filling in a 2½- to 3-quart gratin dish or other shallow baking dish and pipe potatoes decoratively in mounds on filling. *Potpie may be prepared up to this point 1 day ahead and cooled completely, uncovered, before being chilled, loosely covered.*

Bake potpie in middle of oven until filling is bubbling and potatoes are golden on edges, about 30 minutes.

Serves 6.

Photo on page 84

WATERCRESS, FRISÉE, AND PARSLEY SALAD WITH BUTTERMILK DRESSING

FOR DRESSING

    ⅓ cup well-shaken buttermilk

    ¼ cup mayonnaise

    2 teaspoons Dijon mustard, or to taste

    1 teaspoon fresh lemon juice

    1 teaspoon honey

    ¼ teaspoon dried tarragon or to taste, crumbled

    1 head frisée* (French curly endive), torn into pieces

    2 bunches watercress, coarse stems discarded

    1 cup packed fresh flat-leafed parsley leaves

    3 tablespoons dry-roasted sunflower seeds

    * available at specialty produce markets and some supermarkets

Make dressing:

In a small bowl whisk together dressing ingredients and salt and pepper to taste until smooth.

In a large bowl toss *frisée*, watercress, and parsley with dressing and sprinkle with sunflower seeds.

Serves 6.

Apple Pie

=

2 recipes pastry dough (recipe follows)

3 pounds McIntosh apples (about 8)

¾ cup plus 1 tablespoon sugar

2 tablespoons all-purpose flour

1 teaspoon cinnamon

¼ teaspoon freshly grated nutmeg

¼ teaspoon salt

1 tablespoon fresh lemon juice

*2 tablespoons cold unsalted butter,
    cut into bits*

milk for brushing crust

Preheat oven to 450° F.

On a lightly floured surface with a floured rolling pin roll out half of dough ⅛ inch thick. Fit dough into a 9-inch (1-quart capacity) glass pie plate and trim edge, leaving a ¾-inch overhang. Chill shell and remaining dough while making filling.

Peel and core apples and cut into eighths. In a large bowl toss together apples, ¾ cup sugar, flour, spices, salt, and lemon juice until combined well. Transfer filling to shell and dot with butter.

On a lightly floured surface roll out remaining dough into a 13- to 14-inch round. Drape dough over filling and trim it, leaving a 1-inch overhang. Fold overhang under bottom crust, pressing edge to seal, and crimp decoratively. Brush crust lightly with milk and with a sharp knife cut slits for steam vents. Sprinkle pie evenly with remaining tablespoon sugar.

Bake pie on a large baking sheet in middle of oven 20 minutes. Reduce temperature to 350° F. and bake pie 20 minutes more, or until crust is golden and apples are tender. Cool pie on a rack. *Pie may be made 1 day ahead and kept, loosely covered, at room temperature.*

Photo opposite

Pastry Dough

=

1¼ cups all-purpose flour

*¾ stick (6 tablespoons) cold unsalted butter,
    cut into bits*

2 tablespoons cold vegetable shortening

¼ teaspoon salt

2 to 4 tablespoons ice water

In a bowl with a pastry blender or in a food processor blend or pulse together flour, butter, shortening, and salt until mixture resembles coarse meal. Add 2 tablespoons ice water and toss or pulse until incorporated. Add remaining ice water, 1 tablespoon at a time, tossing with a fork or pulsing to incorporate, until mixture begins to form a dough. On a work surface smear dough in 3 or 4 forward motions with heel of hand to make dough easier to work with. Form dough into a ball and flatten to form a disk. *Chill dough, wrapped in plastic wrap, 1 hour.*

Makes enough dough for a single-crust 9- to 10-inch pie.

When you have sleep-over guests and no pressing plans, why not treat everyone to buttermilk waffles and a few extras? If you make the compote a day ahead (and get out the waffle-iron and blender the night before) this little breakfast is easy to prepare. The waffle batter can be whisked together in minutes and cooked as the bacon roasts. Take care to gently cook and warm up the fruit compote; since it's made with arrowroot, a delicate thickener, this topping will turn runny if boiled. The smoothies are a luscious eye-opener that will surely become a favorite snack food or pick-me-up. Just remember to keep a few cut-up bananas in your freezer and vanilla yogurt and apricot nectar on hand. A bit of candied ginger adds peppery sweetness.

◆ Compote may be made 1 day ahead.

◆ Bananas for smoothies must be frozen at least 1 hour.

A LAZY MORNING BREAKFAST

BUTTERMILK WAFFLES

===

3 cups all-purpose flour

1 tablespoon baking powder

¾ teaspoon baking soda

1 teaspoon salt

3¼ cups well-shaken buttermilk

1½ sticks (¾ cup) unsalted butter,
    melted and cooled

3 large eggs, beaten lightly

ACCOMPANIMENT: *apple and dried-fruit compote
    (recipe follows)*

Preheat a well-seasoned or non-stick Belgian or standard waffle iron. Preheat oven to 200° F.

In a large bowl whisk together flour, baking powder, baking soda, and salt and stir in buttermilk, butter, and eggs until smooth (batter will be thick).

Spoon batter into waffle iron, using ½ cup batter for a 4-inch square Belgian waffle or ¼ cup batter for a 4-inch square standard waffle and spreading batter evenly, and cook according to manufacturer's instructions. Transfer waffle to a baking sheet and keep warm, uncovered, in middle of oven. Make more waffles with remaining batter in same manner.

Serve waffles with compote.

Makes about 12 Belgian waffles or about 24 standard waffles, serving 6 generously.

Photo on page 90

APPLE AND DRIED-FRUIT COMPOTE

 ===

3 medium Golden Delicious apples
    (about 1½ pounds total)

1 cup sugar

½ cup dried sour cherries (about 4 ounces)

¼ cup golden raisins

¼ cup dried currants

1½ cups cranberry-raspberry juice

4 teaspoons arrowroot

1 tablespoon fresh lemon juice

Peel and core apples and cut into ¾-inch-thick wedges. In a large saucepan bring apples, sugar, cherries, raisins, currants, and 1¼ cups cranberry-raspberry juice to a boil, stirring occasionally. Simmer compote until apples are just tender, about 1 minute, and remove pan from heat.

In a small bowl stir together arrowroot and remaining ¼ cup cranberry-raspberry juice and stir into compote. Cook compote over moderately low heat, stirring gently, until liquid is thickened and clear (do not boil). *Compote may be prepared up to this point 1 day ahead and cooled, uncovered, before being chilled, covered. Reheat compote over low heat, stirring gently, (do not boil) before pro-ceeding.* Stir lemon juice into compote.

Makes about 5 cups.

Photo on page 90

BROWN SUGAR ROASTED CANADIAN BACON HASH

 =

a ¾-pound piece Canadian bacon,
    cut into ½-inch cubes
2 tablespoons packed brown sugar
⅛ teaspoon ground allspice
2 teaspoons cider vinegar

Preheat oven to 450° F. and grease a shallow
baking dish.

In baking dish toss together all ingredients. Bake hash in middle of oven 15 minutes,
or until most of liquid is evaporated.

Serves 6.

BANANA APRICOT SMOOTHIES

=

2 *large bananas*
3 *cups vanilla yogurt*
¾ *cup apricot nectar, chilled*
2 *teaspoons chopped candied ginger
    (crystallized gingerroot)*

Peel bananas and cut into ½-inch pieces.
*Freeze bananas in one layer in plastic bags
until firm, about 1 hour.*

In a blender purée bananas with
remaining ingredients until smooth.

Serves 6.

CORIANDER LIME SHRIMP

HERBED CHEDDAR AND SUN-DRIED
TOMATO QUESADILLAS

BLACK BEAN TART WITH CHILI CRUST

JÍCAMA, CARROT, AND PEPPERONI
SALAD WITH SALSA VINAIGRETTE

STRAWBERRY MARGARITA
ICE-CREAM PARFAITS

*Dry Creek Vineyard Clarksburg
Dry Chenin Blanc 1996*

SERVES 6

Colorful and inviting, this innovative kitchen party is filled with Southwestern flavor. While the menu may look daunting at first, most dishes can be assembled in stages. Both the shrimp and the quesadillas, for example, can be prepared in advance and require only a few minutes of cooking time. And the black bean tart is delicious warm or at room temperature, so you can pop it in the oven before your guests arrive. When it comes time for the ice-cream parfaits, let everyone make their own dessert.

• Black Bean Tart: The dried beans may be prepared 1 day ahead. (Alternatively, use rinsed canned black beans.) Both the crust and lime sour cream may be prepared 1 day ahead.

• Ice-cream parfaits: Strawberries must macerate at least 1 hour and up to 8 hours. Ice cream must be flavored with lime juice and refrozen 2 hours.

• Quesadillas may be assembled 4 hours ahead.

FESTIVE WEEKEND DINNER

CORIANDER LIME SHRIMP

$1/4$ cup orange marmalade

$1/2$ cup fresh lime juice

3 large garlic cloves, minced and mashed to a
paste with 1 teaspoon salt

$1/2$ cup fresh coriander sprigs, chopped fine

3 tablespoons olive oil

1 tablespoon soy sauce

$1/2$ teaspoon dried hot red pepper flakes

1 pound large shrimp (about 24), shelled,
leaving tail and first shell segment intact,
and if desired deveined

GARNISH: *fresh coriander sprigs*

In a small bowl whisk together marmalade, lime juice, garlic paste, coriander, 2 tablespoons oil, soy sauce, red pepper flakes, and salt and pepper to taste and reserve $1/3$ cup in a ramekin for dipping sauce. In a large sealable plastic bag combine shrimp with remaining mixture and marinate, chilled, tossing occasionally to coat shrimp, 45 minutes.

Drain shrimp and pat dry between paper towels. In a large non-stick skillet heat $1/2$ teaspoons oil over moderately high heat until hot but not smoking and sauté half of shrimp until golden brown and cooked through, about $1/2$ minutes on each side. Transfer cooked shrimp to a platter and sauté remaining shrimp in remaining $1/2$ teaspoons oil in same manner.

Garnish shrimp with coriander sprigs and serve with reserved dipping sauce.

Makes about 24 hors d'oeuvres.

Photo on front jacket

HERBED CHEDDAR AND SUN-DRIED TOMATO QUESADILLAS

eight 7- to 8-inch or four 10-inch flour
tortillas

2 cups coarsely grated Cheddar
(about 8 ounces)

1 tablespoon minced fresh parsley leaves

1 tablespoon minced scallion

2 teaspoons minced fresh oregano leaves

3 tablespoons finely chopped drained bottled
sun-dried tomatoes packed in oil

2 to 3 tablespoons vegetable oil
for brushing tortillas

Preheat broiler.

Arrange half of tortillas in one layer on a large baking sheet. Divide Cheddar, parsley, scallion, oregano, and tomatoes among them and top with remaining tortillas. *Quesadillas may be prepared up to this point 4 hours ahead and chilled, wrapped well in plastic wrap.*

Brush tops lightly with oil and broil *quesadillas* about 2 inches from heat until tops are golden and crisp, about 1 minute. Turn *quesadillas* carefully with a spatula and brush tops lightly with oil. Broil *quesadillas* until tops are golden and crisp, about 1 minute more.

Serve *quesadillas* cut into wedges.

Serves 6 as an hors d'oeuvre.

Black Bean Tart

═══

FOR CRUST

> 1¼ cups all-purpose flour
>
> 1 teaspoon ground cumin
>
> 1 teaspoon chili powder
>
> 1 teaspoon paprika
>
> ½ teaspoon salt
>
> 1 stick (½ cup) cold unsalted butter,
>   cut into bits
>
> 2 tablespoons ice water
>
> raw rice for weighting crust

> ½ pound dried black beans, picked over,
>   or 3 cups canned black beans,
>   rinsed and drained
>
> 1 bay leaf and 1 medium red onion, chopped,
>   if using dried beans
>
> 2 tablespoons sour cream
>
> 1 tablespoon vegetable oil
>
> a 10-ounce package frozen corn, thawed
>
> 1 red bell pepper, chopped
>
> ½ cup fresh coriander sprigs, chopped
>
> 1½ cups coarsely grated Monterey Jack
>
> 2 fresh jalapeño chilies, seeded and chopped
>   fine (wear rubber gloves)
>
> ½ cup chopped scallions (about 2)

ACCOMPANIMENT: *lime sour cream (page 98)*

Make crust:

Preheat oven to 350° F.

In a food processor pulse together flour, spices, and salt until combined well. Add butter and pulse until mixture resembles coarse meal. Add ice water and pulse until incorporated and mixture forms a dough.

Press dough evenly onto bottom and up side of a 10-inch tart pan with a removable fluted rim and chill 15 minutes, or until firm. Line crust with foil and fill with rice. Bake crust in middle of oven 8 to 10 minutes, or until edge is set. Carefully remove foil and rice and bake crust 10 minutes more, or until golden. Cool crust in pan on a rack. *Crust may be made 1 day ahead and kept, covered loosely with plastic wrap, at room temperature.*

If using dried beans: In a bowl soak in water to cover by 2 inches overnight or quick-soak (procedure on page 98) and drain. In a large saucepan combine soaked beans, bay leaf, onion, and water to cover by 2 inches and simmer, uncovered, adding more water if necessary, 1 to 1¼ hours, or until tender. Drain beans, discarding bay leaf, and cool. *Beans may be cooked 1 day ahead and chilled, covered.*

Preheat oven to 350° F.

In a food processor purée 1 cup cooked or canned beans with sour cream until smooth and season with salt and pepper.

In a skillet heat oil over moderately high heat until hot but not smoking and sauté corn with salt and pepper to taste, stirring, 2 minutes. Cool corn. In a large bowl stir together corn, whole beans, bell pepper, coriander, Monterey Jack, *jalapeños*, scallions, and salt and pepper to taste.

Spread bean purée evenly in crust and mound with corn mixture, pressing gently. Bake tart in middle of oven 20 minutes, or until hot and cheese is melted. Cool tart in pan on a rack 15 minutes.

Remove rim of pan and serve tart warm or at room temperature with lime sour cream.

Serves 6.

Photo on page 94

LIME SOUR CREAM

1 cup sour cream

2 teaspoons fresh lime juice, or to taste

In a bowl whisk together sour cream, lime juice, and salt and pepper to taste. *Sauce may be made 1 day ahead and chilled, covered.*

Makes about 1 cup.

TO QUICK-SOAK DRIED BEANS

In a large saucepan combine dried beans, picked over, with triple their volume of cold water. Bring water to a boil and cook beans, uncovered, over moderate heat 2 minutes. Remove pan from heat. Soak beans 1 hour.

Jícama, Carrot, and Pepperoni Salad with Salsa Vinaigrette

===

1/3 cup bottled mild salsa

1 tablespoon red- or white-wine vinegar

2 tablespoons vegetable oil

2 cups shredded iceberg lettuce

2 large carrots, peeled and cut into julienne strips (about 2 cups)

1/2 pound jícama*, peeled and cut into julienne strips (about 2 cups)

2 ounces sliced pepperoni, cut into thin strips

* available at specialty produce markets and some supermarkets

In a blender blend together salsa, vinegar, and oil until combined but not smooth. In a bowl toss together remaining ingredients, salsa vinaigrette, and salt and pepper to taste until combined well.

Serves 6.

Strawberry Margarita Ice-Cream Parfaits

===

1 quart strawberries, quartered

2 tablespoons Cointreau or other orange-flavored liqueur

2 tablespoons sugar

1/3 cup fresh lime juice

1 quart premium vanilla ice cream, softened slightly

Garnish: *fresh lime zest, cut into thin strips*

In a bowl stir together strawberries, liqueur, and sugar. *Macerate strawberries, covered and chilled, at least 1 hour and up to 8 hours.*

In a large bowl stir lime juice into ice cream. *Refreeze ice cream until firm, about 2 hours.* In 6 chilled wineglasses or parfait glasses layer large spoonfuls of ice cream and strawberries, alternating them.

Garnish parfaits with zest.

Serves 6.

You'll want to save this lively menu until your garden (or local farmstand) is brimming with summer's bounty: aromatic fresh basil, delicate zucchini blossoms, crunchy bell peppers, sweet corn, plump tomatoes, and succulent peaches and plums. In particular, for peak freshness and flavor, try to pick zucchini blossoms and corn the morning of your party. For a pretty presentation, pass the fried vegetables in baskets lined with colorful kitchen towels.

◆ Goat cheese spread must be chilled at least 2 hours and up to 1 week.

◆ Peaches and Plums with Honey-Nut Praline: Praline may be made 6 hours ahead. The fruit mixture improves if made 1 hour ahead.

◆ Batter for Fried Zucchini Blossoms and Bell Pepper Rings must be made 1 hour ahead.

FRIED ZUCCHINI BLOSSOMS AND
BELL PEPPER RINGS

CORN, TOMATO, AND
BASIL CHOWDER

GOAT CHEESE SPREAD WITH
GARLIC AND GREEN PEPPERCORNS

PEACHES AND PLUMS WITH
HONEY-NUT PRALINE

*Handley Dry Creek Valley
Sauvignon Blanc 1995*

SERVES 6

FRESH FROM THE GARDEN LUNCH

FRIED ZUCCHINI BLOSSOMS AND BELL PEPPER RINGS

===

1 cup beer (not dark)

¾ cup plus 2 to 3 tablespoons all-purpose flour

⅓ cup packed fresh basil leaves

½ teaspoon salt

vegetable oil for deep-frying

1 large yellow bell pepper, cut into 6 rings

1 large green bell pepper, cut into 6 rings

6 zucchini blossoms*, rinsed and patted dry

GARNISH: 6 fresh basil sprigs

* available seasonally at specialty produce markets and farmers markets

In a blender or food processor blend beer, ¾ cup plus 2 tablespoons flour, basil, and salt 5 seconds. Turn off motor and scrape down side of bowl. Blend batter 20 seconds more, or until just smooth. (Batter should be consistency of pancake batter. If it is too thin, add remaining tablespoon flour and blend 5 seconds more.) Transfer batter to a bowl. *Let batter stand, covered, at room temperature 1 hour.*

Preheat oven to 225° F. and line 2 baking sheets with paper towels.

In a large deep skillet heat 2 inches oil over moderately high heat to 375° F. on a deep-fat thermometer. Stir batter to combine. Working in batches, dip bell pepper rings in batter, letting excess drip off, and fry, without crowding, turning once, until golden, about 1½ minutes. (Make sure oil returns to 375° F. before adding each batch.) Transfer rings as fried with tongs to baking sheets and keep warm in oven. Coat zucchini blossoms and fry in same manner until golden, about 1 minute. Transfer blossoms with tongs as fried to baking sheets and keep warm.

Serve rings and blossoms warm, garnished with basil.

Serves 6.

Photo opposite

CORN, TOMATO, AND BASIL CHOWDER

1 large potato
4 bacon slices
1 large onion, chopped
2 celery ribs, chopped
6 cups chicken broth
4 cups corn (cut from about 8 ears)
½ teaspoon dried thyme, crumbled
1 bay leaf
1 teaspoon salt
1 cup half-and-half
1 large vine-ripened tomato, seeded
   and chopped
½ cup chopped fresh basil leaves

Peel potato and cut into ¼-inch dice. In a heavy kettle cook bacon over moderate heat until crisp and transfer with a slotted spatula to paper towels to drain. In bacon drippings remaining in kettle cook onion and celery over moderately low heat, stirring, until softened. Add broth, corn, thyme, bay leaf, salt, and potato and simmer, covered, 15 minutes, or until vegetables are just tender. Discard bay leaf and transfer 2 cups of solids with a slotted spoon to a blender. Add half-and-half to blender and purée mixture. Add purée, tomato, and basil to chowder and heat, stirring occasionally, until hot (do not boil). Season chowder with salt and pepper.

Crumble bacon and serve chowder topped with it.

Makes about 9 cups, serving 6.

Goat Cheese Spread with Garlic and Green Peppercorns

=

7 ounces soft mild goat cheese at room temperature

3 ounces cream cheese, softened

1 tablespoon drained bottled green peppercorns

1 garlic clove, minced and mashed to a paste with ¼ teaspoon salt

3 tablespoons chopped fresh flat-leafed parsley

ACCOMPANIMENT: *one baguette, sliced thin*

In a food processor blend all ingredients until combined well and transfer to a crock or ramekin. *Chill spread, covered, at least 2 hours and up to 1 week.*

Serve spread with *baguette* slices.

Makes about 1¼ cups.

Peaches and Plums with Honey-Nut Praline

=

5 peaches, peeled if desired and cut into ½-inch wedges

6 plums, cut into ½-inch wedges

⅓ cup sparkling cider

⅓ cup sugar

1 tablespoon freshly grated orange zest

1 tablespoon peach schnapps if desired

FOR HONEY-NUT PRALINE

½ cup coarsely chopped almonds, pecans, hazelnuts, and/or cashews

3 tablespoons honey

½ tablespoon butter

⅛ teaspoon salt

In a bowl gently toss together peaches, plums, cider, sugar, zest, and peach schnapps, if using. *Chill fruit mixture, covered, tossing occasionally, 1 hour.*

Make praline:

In a dry heavy saucepan cook praline ingredients over moderately high heat, stirring, 2 minutes, or until golden. Pour mixture onto a sheet of heavy-duty foil, spreading evenly with a fork, and cool completely, about 20 minutes. Carefully peel off foil and break praline into small pieces. *Praline may be made 6 hours ahead.*

Serve fruit sprinkled with praline pieces.

Serves 6.

Our hearty brunch is the perfect prelude to an afternoon of strolling along country lanes or hiking. The strata may be assembled the night before, leaving you free to put finishing touches on the other dishes. Bake the kielbasa alongside the strata—just remember to start the strata 15 minutes beforehand. Melon, peeled and cut into wedges, makes a quick finale—honeydew, cantaloupe, and casaba are some delicious choices. Choose melons that are fragrant at their blossom ends and weighty for their size; let them fully ripen on your countertop at room temperature.

◆ Onion and Bell Pepper Strata: strata must be assembled at least 3 hours and up to 12 hours ahead. Salsa may be made 2 hours ahead. (Or use store-bought salsa.)

◆ White Sangría may be prepared, in part, 2 hours ahead. Add seltzer and ginger ale just before serving.

BRUNCH BEFORE A COUNTRY STROLL

White Sangría

$^1/_3$ cup fresh lemon juice

$^1/_3$ cup fresh lime juice

1 cup fresh orange juice

a 750-ml. bottle dry white wine, chilled

$^1/_2$ cup Pimm's No. 1 Cup

1 navel orange, cut into wedges

1 lemon, cut into wedges

1 cup seltzer or club soda

$1^1/_2$ cups ginger ale

In a large pitcher or bowl stir together citrus juices, wine, Pimm's, and half of orange and lemon wedges. *Sangría may be prepared up to this point 2 hours ahead and chilled, covered.*

Add seltzer or club soda, ginger ale, and ice cubes and serve sangría with remaining orange and lemon wedges.

Makes about 8 cups, serving 6.

Photo on page 106

Onion and Bell Pepper Strata with Fresh Tomato Salsa

1 medium onion, sliced thin

$1^1/_2$ tablespoons minced garlic

$^1/_2$ tablespoon olive oil

1 large green bell pepper, sliced thin

1 large yellow bell pepper, sliced thin

12 very thin slices firm white sandwich bread, cut into $^3/_4$-inch squares (about 5 cups)

$^1/_2$ cup freshly grated Parmesan (about $1^1/_2$ ounces)

4 whole large eggs

4 large egg whites

$2^1/_2$ cups milk

$^1/_2$ cup packed fresh parsley leaves, chopped fine

ACCOMPANIMENT: **tomato salsa (recipe follows)**

Lightly oil a 13- by 9- by 2-inch baking dish (about 3-quart capacity).

In a large non-stick skillet cook onion and 1 tablespoon garlic in oil over moderate heat, stirring, until onion is pale golden. Stir in bell peppers and salt and pepper to taste and cook, covered, over moderately low heat 5 minutes, or until peppers are just tender. Remove lid and cook vegetables, stirring, until any excess liquid is evaporated, 2 to 3 minutes.

Spread half of bread squares evenly in baking dish and top with half of vegetables. Sprinkle $^1/_4$ cup Parmesan evenly over vegetables and top with remaining bread and vegetables.

In a bowl whisk together whole eggs, whites, milk, parsley, remaining $^1/_2$ tablespoon garlic, and salt and pepper to taste and pour evenly over bread and vegetables. *Chill strata, covered, at least 3 hours and up to 12.*

Preheat oven to 375° F. and let *strata* stand at room temperature 20 minutes.

Sprinkle remaining $^1/_4$ cup Parmesan over *strata* and bake in middle of oven 45 to 55 minutes, or until puffed and golden brown around edges.

Serve *strata* topped with salsa.

Serves 6.

Photo on page 106

Tomato Salsa

1 $^1/_2$ pounds vine-ripened tomatoes (about 5 medium), seeded and chopped coarse

$^1/_2$ cup finely chopped onion

2 scallions, chopped fine

$^1/_2$ cup packed fresh coriander sprigs, chopped fine

1 tablespoon fresh lemon or lime juice

Tabasco to taste if desired

In a bowl stir together all ingredients. *Tomato salsa may be made 2 hours ahead and chilled, covered.*

Makes about 3 cups.

Roasted Kielbasa with Horseradish Apple Sour Cream

1 pound kielbasa or other ready-to-eat smoked sausage

$^1/_3$ cup balsamic vinegar

1 sweet or tart apple

$^1/_2$ cup sour cream

2 teaspoons drained bottled horseradish, or to taste

Preheat oven to 375° F.

Cut *kielbasa* diagonally into $^1/_2$-inch-thick slices and arrange in a baking pan large enough to hold them in one layer. Pour vinegar over slices. Bake *kielbasa* in middle of oven, turning once, 30 minutes, or until browned.

Peel apple and coarsely grate enough to measure $^1/_4$ cup. In a small bowl stir together apple, sour cream, and horseradish.

Serve *kielbasa* with a dollop of horseradish apple sour cream on the side.

Serves 6.

ROASTED BUTTERNUT SQUASH,
ROSEMARY, AND GARLIC LASAGNE

SPINACH SALAD WITH
SHERRY VINAIGRETTE

CRUSTY BREAD (STORE-BOUGHT)

GINGER CAKE WITH
CARAMELIZED PEARS

*Ponzi Willamette Valley
Pinot Gris 1995*

SERVES 6

This menu sparkles with dressed-up favorites that are sure to please. The lasagne, redolent of fresh rosemary and garlic, is heavenly and creamy, and spinach salad provides a tart, refreshing contrast. No-boil lasagne makes our pasta dish a breeze to assemble. Just be sure to completely cover the top or it will dry out. For dessert, we've chosen the ultimate comfort food: a ginger cake enlivened with a bite of fresh ginger.

To serve a square cake in triangular pieces: Cut cake in half, divide each half crosswise in thirds, then cut each rectangle on the diagonal.

◆ Sauce for the lasagne may be made 3 days ahead.

◆ Ginger Cake with Caramelized Pears: Caramelized pears may be made 1 day ahead. Ginger cake may be made 6 hours ahead.

CONTEMPORARY
VEGETARIAN SUPPER

Roasted Butternut Squash, Rosemary, and Garlic Lasagne

====

3 pounds butternut squash, quartered, seeded,
   peeled, and cut into $1/2$-inch cubes
   (about $9^1/2$ cups)

3 tablespoons vegetable oil

4 cups milk

2 tablespoons dried rosemary, crumbled

1 tablespoon minced garlic

$1/2$ stick ($1/4$ cup) unsalted butter

$1/4$ cup all-purpose flour

nine 7- by $3^1/2$-inch sheets dried no-boil
   lasagne

$1^1/3$ cups freshly grated Parmesan
   (about 5 ounces)

1 cup heavy cream

$1/2$ teaspoon salt

GARNISH: *fresh rosemary sprigs*

Preheat oven to 450° F. and oil 2 large shallow baking pans.

In a large bowl toss squash with oil until well coated and spread in one layer in pans. Roast squash 10 minutes and season with salt. Stir squash and roast 10 minutes more, or until tender and beginning to turn golden.

While squash is roasting, in a saucepan bring milk with rosemary to a simmer. Cook milk mixture over low heat 10 minutes and pour through a sieve into a large heatproof 1-quart pitcher or measuring cup.

In a large heavy saucepan cook garlic in butter over moderately low heat, stirring, until softened. Stir in flour and cook *roux*, stirring, 3 minutes. Remove pan from heat and add milk mixture in a stream, whisking until smooth. Simmer sauce, whisking occasionally, 10 minutes, or until thickened. Stir in squash and salt and pepper to taste. *Sauce may be made 3 days ahead and chilled, its surface covered with plastic wrap.*

Reduce temperature to 375° F. and butter a 13- by 9- by 2-inch baking dish.

Pour 1 cup sauce into baking dish (sauce will not cover bottom completely) and cover with 3 lasagne sheets, making sure they do not touch. Spread half of remaining sauce over pasta and sprinkle with $1/2$ cup Parmesan. Make 1 more layer in same manner with 3 lasagne sheets, remaining sauce, and $1/2$ cup Parmesan and top with remaining 3 lasagne sheets.

In a bowl with an electric mixer beat cream with salt until it holds soft peaks and spread evenly over lasagne, making sure pasta is completely covered. Sprinkle remaining $1/3$ cup Parmesan over cream. Cover dish tightly with foil, tenting slightly to prevent foil from touching cream, and bake in middle of oven 30 minutes. Remove foil and bake lasagne 10 minutes more, or until bubbling and golden. Let lasagne stand 5 minutes.

Garnish each serving with a rosemary sprig.

Serves 6.

Photo on page 110

Spinach Salad

2 tablespoons Sherry vinegar

1 teaspoon Dijon mustard

1 teaspoon honey

6 tablespoons extra-virgin olive oil

1½ pounds spinach, stems discarded and
    leaves washed, dried, and torn into pieces

½ pound mushrooms, sliced

1 red onion, halved lengthwise and sliced thin

In a large bowl whisk together vinegar, mustard, honey, and salt and pepper to taste and add oil in a stream, whisking until emulsified. Add remaining ingredients and toss.

Serves 6.

Ginger Cake with Caramelized Pears

1½ sticks (¾ cup) unsalted butter

½ cup unsulfured molasses

½ cup sour cream

½ cup packed light brown sugar

2 large eggs

4 teaspoons finely grated peeled fresh
    gingerroot

1 teaspoon freshly grated lemon zest

2 cups all-purpose flour

1 teaspoon baking soda

½ teaspoon salt

4 medium firm-ripe pears

2 tablespoons fresh lemon juice

½ cup granulated sugar

⅓ cup water

¼ cup Cognac or other brandy

⅓ cup heavy cream

Preheat oven to 350° F. and butter and flour a 9-inch square baking pan.

In a small saucepan melt 1 stick butter. In a bowl whisk together melted butter, molasses, sour cream, brown sugar, eggs, gingerroot, and zest until smooth and sift in flour, baking soda, and salt. Stir batter until just combined and spread evenly in baking pan.

Bake cake in oven 25 minutes, or until a tester comes out clean. Cool cake in pan on a rack 5 minutes and turn out onto rack.

Peel pears and cut each lengthwise into 6 wedges, discarding cores. In a small bowl toss pears with lemon juice. In a heavy skillet large enough to hold pears in one layer melt remaining ½ stick butter over moderate heat and cook pears, shaking skillet, 3 minutes. Sprinkle pears with granulated sugar and cook, shaking skillet and turning pears, until sugar is melted and pears are tender. Transfer pears with a slotted spoon to bowl.

Boil sugar mixture remaining in skillet, stirring occasionally and swirling skillet, until it begins to turn a golden caramel. Remove skillet from heat and carefully add water, brandy, and cream (mixture will bubble up). Simmer sauce, stirring, until smooth and slightly thickened. Return pears to skillet and cook until heated through.

Serve cake warm or at room temperature with caramelized pears.

An early evening hors d'oeuvres party must be substantial enough to serve as dinner—and we can assure you, ours is! We've taken our cue from Mediterranean lands where a collection of mezze (appetizers) are frequently offered as a casual supper.

◆ Roasted Red Peppers with Anchovy, Caper, and Herb Dressing must marinate 3 hours and up to 3 days.

◆ White bean salad may be made 1 day ahead. Just before serving, spoon salad into lettuce cups.

◆ Pistachio torte may be prepared 1 day ahead and left unglazed. Glaze and garnish the torte about 1 hour before serving.

◆ Lamb for the kebabs must marinate at least 1 hour and up to 8 hours.

SPINACH PHYLLO PIZZA

ROASTED PEPPERS WITH ANCHOVY, CAPER, AND HERB DRESSING

GRILLED LAMB KEBABS

WHITE BEAN, ORANGE, AND OLIVE SALAD IN LETTUCE CUPS

PISTACHIO TORTE WITH LEMON CARDAMOM GLAZE

Zaca Mesa Z Cuvée
Santa Barbara County Red Wine 1994

SERVES 6 TO 8

MEDITERRANEAN HORS D'OEUVRES BUFFET

Spinach Phyllo Pizza

—

1½ *pounds spinach (about 2 bunches), coarse*
  stems discarded and leaves washed well
  and drained

For phyllo crust

  5 *tablespoons unsalted butter, melted and*
    kept warm

  seven 17- by 12-inch phyllo sheets, thawed if
    frozen, stacked between 2 sheets plastic
    wrap and covered with a kitchen towel

  6 *tablespoons freshly grated Parmesan*

  1 *tablespoon finely chopped fresh mint leaves*
  ½ *cup very thinly sliced red onion*
  ⅔ *cup finely crumbled feta*
  1½ *tablespoons extra-virgin olive oil*

In a kettle cook spinach in water clinging to leaves, covered, over moderate heat until just wilted, about 3 minutes, and drain in a colander. Rinse spinach under cold water to stop cooking and drain well.

Make *phyllo* crust:

Preheat oven to 400° F. and brush a baking sheet lightly with some butter.

Put 1 *phyllo* sheet on baking sheet and brush lightly with butter. Sprinkle sheet with 1 tablespoon Parmesan and top with another *phyllo* sheet, pressing firmly to adhere to bottom layer. Continue to layer remaining *phyllo* sheets with butter and Parmesan in same manner, ending with a *phyllo* sheet. Brush top sheet with remaining butter and bake crust in middle of oven 5 minutes.

Gently squeeze spinach dry and arrange evenly on crust, leaving a 1-inch border all around. Sprinkle mint over spinach and season with salt and pepper. Scatter onion and feta over spinach and drizzle with oil.

Bake pizza in middle of oven 15 minutes, or until cheese is melted.

With a pizza wheel or sharp knife cut pizza into squares.

Serves 6 to 8 as part of a buffet.

Photo on page 114

To Roast Peppers

═══

Gas stove method:

Lay peppers on their sides on racks of burners (preferably 1 to a burner) and turn flame on high. Char peppers, turning them with tongs, until skins are blackened, 6 to 8 minutes. (If peppers are small, spear through stem end with a long-handled fork and rest pepper on burner rack.)

Transfer peppers to a bowl and let stand, covered, until cool enough to handle. Peel peppers. Cut off tops and discard seeds and ribs.

Broiler method:

Preheat broiler.

Broil peppers on rack of a broiler pan about 2 inches from heat, turning them every 5 minutes, until skins are blistered and charred, 15 to 20 minutes.

Transfer peppers to a bowl and let stand, covered, until cool enough to handle. Peel peppers. Cut off tops and discard seeds and ribs.

ROASTED PEPPERS WITH ANCHOVY, CAPER, AND HERB DRESSING

===

FOR DRESSING

$^1/_3$ cup extra-virgin olive oil

1 tablespoon white-wine vinegar, or to taste

3 tablespoons minced fresh oregano leaves or 2 teaspoons dried oregano, crumbled

3 tablespoons chopped fresh basil leaves

4 anchovy fillets, rinsed, patted dry, and chopped

$^1/_4$ cup rinsed drained capers, chopped coarse

6 large red bell peppers, roasted and peeled (procedure opposite)

Make dressing:

In a large bowl whisk together dressing ingredients and season with salt and pepper.

Cut each bell pepper lengthwise into eighths and add to dressing, tossing to coat well. *Marinate peppers, covered and chilled, at least 3 hours and up to 3 days. Bring peppers to room temperature before serving.*

Serves 6 to 8 as part of a buffet.

GRILLED LAMB KEBABS

===

$1^1/_2$ pounds boneless leg of lamb, cut into 1-inch cubes

1 tablespoon fresh lemon juice

$^1/_2$ teaspoon ground cumin

$^1/_8$ teaspoon cayenne

2 garlic cloves, minced and mashed to a paste with 1 teaspoon salt

3 tablespoons olive oil

twenty-four 6-inch bamboo skewers, soaked in water 1 hour

1 large bunch fresh flat-leafed parsley sprigs for lining platter plus 2 tablespoons minced fresh parsley leaves

ACCOMPANIMENT: **grilled pita loaves, quartered**

In a bowl toss together lamb, lemon juice, spices, garlic paste, and olive oil. *Marinate lamb, covered and chilled, at least 1 hour and up to 8 hours.*

Prepare grill.

Thread about 3 lamb cubes loosely onto each skewer and grill on a well-oiled rack set 5 to 6 inches over glowing coals, turning occasionally, 4 to 6 minutes for medium-rare. (Alternatively, broil lamb on rack of a broiler pan about 4 inches from preheated broiler, turning occasionally, 4 to 6 minutes.)

Arrange skewers on a platter lined with parsley sprigs and sprinkle kebabs with minced parsley. Serve kebabs with grilled pita loaves.

Makes 24 brochettes, serving 6 to 8 as part of a buffet.

White Bean, Orange, and Olive Salad in Lettuce Cups

====

3/4 cup picked-over dried Great Northern or
    other white beans (about 4 ounces)

1 bay leaf

1 1/2 teaspoons fennel seeds, crushed coarse

2 navel oranges

1/2 cup chopped pitted green olives

1/2 cup chopped red onion

1/4 cup chopped fresh parsley leaves

1 garlic clove, minced

1 to 1 1/2 tablespoons fresh lemon juice

2 tablespoons extra-virgin olive oil,
    or to taste

24 small Bibb lettuce leaves

In a large saucepan cover beans with water by 3 inches and add bay leaf and fennel seeds. Gently simmer beans, covered, stirring occasionally, 1 to 1 1/4 hours, or until beans are just tender but not mushy.

Drain beans in a colander, discarding bay leaf, and transfer to a large bowl. Season beans with salt and pepper and cool.

With a sharp knife cut peel and pith from oranges. Cut orange sections free from membranes and cut into 1-inch pieces. Add orange sections to beans with olives, onion, parsley, garlic, lemon juice to taste, and oil. Toss salad and season with salt and pepper. *Salad may be made 1 day ahead and chilled, covered. Bring salad to room temperature before proceeding.*

Spoon 1 tablespoon salad into each lettuce leaf and arrange on a platter.

Makes 24 lettuce cups, serving 6 to 8 as part of a buffet.

PISTACHIO TORTE WITH LEMON CARDAMOM GLAZE

═══

FOR TORTE

 1 cup unsalted shelled natural pistachios

 1 cup granulated sugar

 1/3 cup all-purpose flour

 1 stick (1/2 cup) unsalted butter, melted

 1 teaspoon freshly grated lemon zest

 1 teaspoon vanilla

 1/2 teaspoon almond extract

 3/4 cup egg whites (from about 5 large eggs)

 1/4 teaspoon salt

FOR GLAZE

 1/2 cup confectioners' sugar

 1 tablespoon fresh lemon juice

 1/8 teaspoon ground cardamom

 GARNISH: *2 tablespoons chopped unsalted shelled natural pistachios*

 ACCOMPANIMENT: *vanilla ice cream*

Make torte:

Preheat oven to 375° F. and butter a 9-inch springform pan. Line bottom of pan with a round of wax paper and butter paper.

In a food processor or blender finely grind pistachios with 3/4 cup sugar. Transfer mixture to a large bowl and stir in flour, butter, zest, vanilla, and almond extract. In another bowl with an electric mixer beat whites with salt until they barely hold soft peaks and gradually beat in remaining 1/4 cup sugar until meringue just holds stiff peaks. Stir one third of meringue into pistachio mixture to lighten and fold in remaining meringue gently but thoroughly. Pour batter into pan.

Bake torte in middle of oven 40 minutes, or until it pulls away from side of pan and top is golden brown. Cool torte in pan on a rack 10 minutes. Run a knife around edge of pan and remove side. Invert torte onto rack and remove bottom of pan. Carefully peel off wax paper and cool torte completely. *Torte may be prepared up to this point 1 day ahead and kept, wrapped well in plastic wrap, in an airtight container at room temperature.*

Make glaze:

In a small bowl whisk together glaze ingredients until smooth.

With a spatula spread glaze over top of torte, letting it drip down side.

Garnish top with chopped pistachios and let glaze set. Serve torte with ice cream.

Black-eyed peas, thought to bring good luck when enjoyed on New Year's Day, may just spur your favorite team to victory. In any event, our stew will warm your guests and needs few accompaniments —rice, a green salad, and perhaps our rolls. For dessert we offer two chocolatey options: a dense, rich cake or sweet, nutty cookies.

◆ Sweet-potato rolls may be made 1 week ahead and frozen.

Menu

BLACK-EYED PEA AND HAM STEW

WHITE RICE

GREEN SALAD

SWEET-POTATO CLOVERLEAF ROLLS

▬

CHOCOLATE CHOCOLATE-CHIP
RUM CAKE
OR
CHOCOLATE CHIP PECAN COOKIES

▬

*Davis Bynum Russian River Valley
Laureles Vineyard Merlot 1994*

SERVES 8

◆ **Black-Eyed Pea and Ham Stew:** The stew may be made 3 days ahead and improves in flavor if made at least 1 day ahead. Dried black-eyed peas must soak for 1 hour.

◆ **Chocolate Chip Pecan Cookies:** Baked cookies keep 5 days. Cookie dough must be made at least 1 hour and up to 1 day ahead.

◆ **Chocolate Chocolate-Chip Rum Cake** may be made 3 days ahead.

LUNCH BEFORE THE PLAYOFFS

Black-Eyed Pea and Ham Stew

==

1 pound dried black-eyed peas, picked over

1 smoked ham hock, blanched in boiling
    water 2 minutes and drained

1 cup chopped onion

1 cup chopped green bell pepper

1 cup chopped celery

1$\frac{1}{2}$ pounds cooked ham, cut into 1$\frac{1}{2}$-inch
    pieces

1 bay leaf

8 cups cold water

2 tablespoons ketchup

1 tablespoon Worcestershire sauce

2$\frac{1}{2}$ tablespoons arrowroot

Tabasco to taste

$\frac{1}{2}$ cup minced fresh parsley leaves

$\frac{1}{2}$ cup thinly sliced scallion greens

ACCOMPANIMENT: *cooked white rice*

In a kettle cover peas with cold water by 2 inches and bring to a boil. Boil peas 2 minutes and remove kettle from heat. *Soak peas 1 hour.* In a colander drain peas and rinse well.

In kettle bring peas, ham hock, onion, bell pepper, celery, ham, bay leaf, and 8 cups cold water to a boil and simmer, uncovered, stirring occasionally, 30 minutes. Stir in ketchup and Worcestershire sauce and simmer, uncovered, 15 to 20 minutes, or until peas are tender.

In a small bowl stir together $\frac{1}{2}$ cup hot cooking liquid and arrowroot until arrowroot is dissolved. Stir arrowroot mixture into stew and cook over moderately low heat, stirring, 1 minute, or until thickened. (Do not let stew boil.) *Stew may be prepared up to this point 3 days ahead and cooled, uncovered, before being chilled, covered. Reheat stew over low heat until hot but not boiling before proceeding.*

Discard bay leaf and stir in Tabasco, salt to taste, parsley, and scallion.

Serve stew with white rice.

Serves 8.

Photo on page 120

To Freeze Baked Goods

====

Cool baked goods completely and wrap them, first in plastic wrap, then in heavy-duty foil, before freezing at 0° F.

BREADS AND ROLLS:

Wrap rolls individually. Thaw rolls and bread, wrapped, at room temperature (unless recipe indicates otherwise). Heat hard-crusted breads, very loosely wrapped (remove plastic), in a preheated 400° F. oven 5 minutes to crisp. All breads keep up to 3 months.

CAKES:

Angel food, butter, sponge, and chiffon cakes keep up to 2 months; dense pound cakes keep 4 months. Thaw cakes, wrapped, at room temperature until completely thawed.

SWEET-POTATO CLOVERLEAF ROLLS

==

¼ cup warm water (105° to 115° F.)

a ¼-ounce package (2½ teaspoons) active
    dry yeast

3 tablespoons sugar

2 large eggs

⅓ cup milk

½ stick (¼ cup) unsalted butter, melted and
    cooled, plus additional melted butter for
    brushing rolls

1 teaspoon salt

¾ cup mashed cooked sweet potatoes

3 to 4 cups all-purpose flour

In a small bowl stir together water, yeast, and
1 tablespoon sugar and let stand until foamy,
about 5 minutes. In a large bowl whisk
together eggs, remaining 2 tablespoons sugar,
milk, ½ stick melted butter, salt, sweet potatoes, and yeast mixture until combined well.

Stir in 3 cups flour, 1 cup at a time, and turn
dough out onto a floured surface. Knead
dough, incorporating enough of remaining 1
cup flour to prevent dough from sticking, 8 to
10 minutes, or until smooth and elastic. Form
dough into a ball and transfer to a well-but-
tered large bowl, turning to coat. *Let dough
rise, covered with plastic wrap, in a warm
place 1 hour, or until doubled in bulk.*

Butter eighteen ⅓-cup muffin tins.

Turn dough out onto a floured surface.
Cut off walnut-size pieces of dough and form
into balls. Put 3 balls into each muffin tin
and brush tops with additional melted butter.
Let cloverleaf rolls rise, covered loosely, in a
warm place 30 to 45 minutes, or until almost
doubled in bulk.

Preheat oven to 400° F.

Bake potato rolls in middle of oven 12 to
15 minutes, or until golden. *Rolls may be
made 1 week ahead and frozen, wrapped individually in plastic wrap and foil. Reheat rolls,
wrapped in foil (discard plastic wrap), in a preheated 400° F. oven 25 to 30 minutes, or until
heated through.*

Makes about 18 rolls.

Photo above

CHOCOLATE CHOCOLATE-CHIP RUM CAKE

—

6 ounces unsweetened chocolate, chopped

2¼ sticks unsalted butter, softened

2 cups sugar

4 large eggs at room temperature

2½ cups all-purpose flour

1 teaspoon baking powder

1 teaspoon baking soda

½ teaspoon salt

1 cup well-shaken buttermilk

2 teaspoons vanilla

¼ cup dark rum

1 cup semisweet chocolate chips

ACCOMPANIMENT: whipped cream

Preheat oven to 350° F. Butter and flour a 3-quart *Kugelhupf* pan or bundt pan.

In a double boiler or metal bowl set over a saucepan of barely simmering water melt unsweetened chocolate and ½ stick butter, stirring, until smooth and remove top of double boiler or bowl from heat. Let mixture cool. In a large bowl with an electric mixer beat remaining 1¾ sticks butter until smooth and add sugar, a little at a time, beating until light and fluffy. Add eggs, 1 at a time, beating well after each addition, and beat in chocolate mixture. Into a bowl sift together flour, baking powder, baking soda, and salt and add to egg mixture alternately with buttermilk, beginning and ending with flour mixture and blending well after each addition. Stir in vanilla, rum, and chocolate chips and spoon batter into pan. Rap pan on a hard surface several times to settle batter.

Bake cake in middle of oven 1 hour, or until a skewer comes out clean. Cool cake in pan on a rack 10 minutes. Turn cake out onto rack and cool completely. *Cake may be made 3 days ahead and kept, wrapped well in plastic wrap, in an airtight container at cool room temperature.*

Serve cake with whipped cream.

TO FREEZE DOUGHS

═

COOKIES:

Most cookie doughs freeze well, which we prefer to freezing baked cookies. Form refrigerator cookie dough into a cylinder and wrap well in plastic wrap, then in foil. For rolled cookie dough, cut it into desired shapes and store, in layers separated by wax paper, in an airtight container. Uncut cookie doughs keep 3 months; cut doughs keep 1 month.

PIES AND TARTS:

Freeze pastry dough before filling and baking. Shape dough into a disk and wrap in plastic wrap and foil. Or, roll and fit dough into a pie plate or tart tin, and wrap well in plastic wrap. Thaw frozen doughs, wrapped, at room temperature for at least 2 hours.

CHOCOLATE CHIP PECAN COOKIES

===

½ stick (¼ cup) unsalted butter, softened
¼ cup vegetable shortening
⅓ cup sugar
1 teaspoon vanilla
1 cup all-purpose flour
½ teaspoon salt
¼ teaspoon baking powder
⅓ cup pecans, chopped fine
½ cup mini semisweet chocolate chips

In a bowl with an electric mixer beat together butter, shortening, sugar, and vanilla until light and fluffy. In a bowl whisk together flour, salt, and baking powder. Beat flour mixture and pecans into butter mixture until combined well and stir in chocolate chips until evenly distributed. Form dough into a ball and flatten to form a disk. *Chill dough, wrapped in plastic wrap, at least 1 hour and up to 1 day.*

Preheat oven to 350° F. and grease 2 baking sheets.

Pat out dough ¼-inch thick on a sheet of wax paper. With a 2-inch round cutter cut out rounds and arrange 2 inches apart on baking sheets. Gather and pat out scraps and make more rounds in same manner. (If dough becomes too soft, transfer it on wax paper to a baking sheet and chill until firm.)

Bake cookies in batches in middle of oven 10 to 12 minutes, or until golden. Transfer cookies to racks and cool completely. *Cookies keep in an airtight container at room temperature 5 days.*

Makes about 26 cookies.

Photo on page 70

3

GARDEN PARTIES

A shady courtyard or porch and an easy menu make casual warm-weather entertaining a pleasure. Raspberry vinegar, a surprising and effective marinade ingredient, infuses the chicken with fresh berry flavor that lingers even after grilling. Both side dishes highlight fresh summer harvests—green and wax beans are bathed in a warm Parmesan mustard sauce, while juicy tomatoes moisten a rustic bread salad tossed with fresh basil, garlic, and black olives. Our almond tart, an Italian "crostata" (sweet tart) is irresistible. The pastry dough is sweet, buttery, and tender, perfect for the simple filling made with almonds and cherry or raspberry jam. On very hot, humid days, pat the dough into the tart pan instead of rolling it out.

◆ Almond Tart: Pastry dough may be made 1 day ahead. Tart may be baked 1 day ahead.

◆ Chicken must marinate at least 30 minutes and up to 1½ hours.

RASPBERRY-AND-THYME-MARINATED CHICKEN

TOMATO BREAD SALAD WITH HERBS

GREEN AND WAX BEANS WITH PARMESAN SAUCE

■

ALMOND TART

■

Kunde Sonoma Valley Sauvignon Blanc 1995

SERVES 4

LUNCH IN THE COURTYARD

RASPBERRY-AND-THYME-MARINATED CHICKEN

⸻

⅓ cup raspberry vinegar

1 tablespoon fresh lemon juice

3 scallions, minced

1 teaspoon dried thyme, crumbled

2 whole chicken breasts with skin and bones (about 1¼ pounds total), halved

2 tablespoons olive oil

In a large sealable plastic bag combine all ingredients except oil and seal bag, pressing out excess air. Turn bag to coat chicken well. *Marinate chicken, chilled, at least 30 minutes and up to 1½ hours.*

Prepare grill.

Transfer chicken to a plate, discarding marinade, and brush with oil. Season chicken generously with salt and pepper and grill on an oiled rack set 5 to 6 inches over glowing coals 10 to 15 minutes on each side, or until cooked through.

Serves 4.

TOMATO BREAD SALAD WITH HERBS

2 tablespoons red-wine vinegar

2 garlic cloves, minced and mashed to a paste with a pinch salt

½ cup extra-virgin olive oil

4 cups ¾-inch cubes crusty bread

1 pound vine-ripened red tomatoes, cut into ¾-inch wedges

1 pound vine-ripened yellow tomatoes, cut into ¾-inch wedges

½ cup Niçoise or Kalamata olives, pitted if desired

½ cup fresh basil leaves, chopped fine

2 tablespoons fresh marjoram leaves, chopped fine

In a bowl whisk together vinegar, garlic paste, and pepper to taste and add oil in a stream, whisking until emulsified. Add remaining ingredients and salt to taste and toss to combine well. Let salad stand at room temperature 15 minutes to allow bread to soak up some dressing.

Serves 4.

Photo on page 128

GREEN AND WAX BEANS WITH PARMESAN SAUCE

1 pound green and/or wax beans, trimmed

⅓ cup freshly grated Parmesan

1½ tablespoons cream cheese, softened

1½ teaspoons Dijon mustard

1 garlic clove, minced

3 tablespoons olive oil

1 tablespoon white-wine vinegar

1 tablespoon water

In a large saucepan of boiling salted water simmer beans until crisp-tender, about 5 minutes, and drain.

In a blender blend together Parmesan, cream cheese, mustard, and garlic. In a small saucepan bring oil, vinegar, and water just to a boil. With blender on low speed add hot oil mixture in a stream, blending until thick and creamy. Season sauce with salt and pepper and pour over beans, tossing to coat.

Serves 4.

ALMOND TART

==

Italian sweet pastry dough (recipe follows)
¾ cup cherry or raspberry jam
3 large eggs
¼ cup granulated sugar
a 7-ounce package almond paste
½ cup all-purpose flour
½ cup sliced almonds

GARNISH: *confectioners' sugar for dusting*

Preheat oven to 350° F.

On a lightly floured surface roll out dough ⅛ inch thick. Fit dough into a 9-inch tart pan with a removable fluted rim and trim dough flush with rim. Chill shell 30 minutes. Spread jam on bottom of shell.

In a bowl with an electric mixer beat eggs until foamy and gradually beat in granulated sugar. Crumble almond paste into egg mixture, beating until combined well. Fold in flour gently but thoroughly and spread filling evenly over jam. Sprinkle top with almonds.

Bake tart in lower third of oven 35 to 40 minutes, or until golden and firm in center. Cool tart in pan on a rack 10 minutes. Remove rim and cool tart completely on rack. *Tart may be made 1 day ahead and kept, loosely covered, at cool room temperature.*

Before serving, dust top of tart with confectioners' sugar.

ITALIAN SWEET PASTRY DOUGH

==

1⅓ cups all-purpose flour
3 tablespoons sugar
½ teaspoon salt
freshly grated zest of 1 lemon
1 stick (½ cup) cold unsalted butter,
    cut into bits
1 large egg, beaten lightly
1 teaspoon vanilla

In a bowl whisk together flour, sugar, salt, and zest and with a pastry blender or 2 knives blend in butter until it resembles meal. Add egg and vanilla and toss with a fork until egg is incorporated. On a work surface knead dough lightly with heel of your hand to distribute egg. Form dough into a disk. *Chill dough, wrapped in plastic wrap, at least 1 hour and up to 1 day.* Let dough stand at room temperature until softened but still firm enough to roll out.

Makes enough dough for a 9-inch tart.

A

sian flavors reawaken the senses, making them ideal for our bright springtime dinner. This menu urges you to experiment with varied tastes—sweet, spicy, and sour—and textures—crunchy, tender, and smooth. Our spring rolls are made with delicate rice paper rounds that can be a bit tricky to work with (don't soak them for too long, or they can tear). Short ribs, a tough cut of beef that is usually stewed or braised, are delicious for grilling after a tenderizing marinade in sweet sesame sauce. Our dessert mousses are tinted and subtly flavored with Midori, a bright-green Japanese melon liqueur available in most liquor stores.

◆ Mousses must be chilled at least 1 hour and up to 24 hours.

◆ Short ribs must marinate overnight.

◆ Spring rolls and dipping sauce may be made 6 hours ahead.

◆ Salad may be made 1 hour ahead.

SPRINGTIME ASIAN DINNER

Cold Shrimp and Vegetable Spring Rolls

FOR SAUCE

>6 tablespoons mayonnaise
>
>2 teaspoons seasoned rice vinegar*
>
>1 teaspoon soy sauce
>
>1 pound large shrimp (about 15), shelled and deveined
>
>twelve 6½-inch rounds rice paper*
>
>¾ cup finely shredded iceberg lettuce
>
>1 red bell pepper, cut into matchsticks
>
>¾ cup fresh coriander leaves
>
>¼ cup finely chopped scallion greens
>
>*available at Asian markets and by mail (page 231)

Make sauce:

In a small bowl whisk together sauce ingredients until combined well.

In a saucepan of boiling salted water cook shrimp until just cooked through, 1 to 2 minutes, and drain. Cool shrimp and cut into ¼-inch pieces.

In a shallow baking pan or cake pan soak 3 rounds rice paper in warm water to cover until very pliable, about 45 seconds. Carefully transfer soaked rounds to paper towels to drain, arranging them in one layer. Keeping remaining soaked rounds covered with dampened paper towels, put 1 soaked round on a clean dry work surface and spread a scant teaspoon sauce in a line across bottom, 1 inch from edge. Top sauce with about 1 tablespoon each of lettuce, bell pepper, and coriander, 2 tablespoons shrimp, and 1 teaspoon scallion and season with salt and pepper. Begin rolling up filling tightly in rice paper, folding in sides after first turn to completely enclose filling, and continue rolling.

Make 2 more spring rolls in same manner with remaining soaked rounds. Transfer rolls as assembled to a tray and cover with dampened paper towels. Repeat procedure with remaining 9 rice paper rounds and filling ingredients. Tightly cover tray with plastic wrap (keeping dampened paper towels directly on spring rolls). Transfer sauce to a small bowl and cover with plastic wrap. *Spring rolls and sauce may be made 6 hours ahead and chilled separately.*

Just before serving, halve spring rolls on the diagonal with a sharp knife and serve with remaining sauce.

Makes 24 hors d'oeuvres.

Korean-Style Grilled Short Ribs and Scallions

>six 1½- to 2-inch-thick beef short ribs (sometimes called Flanken), meaty side trimmed of excess fat
>
>5 garlic cloves, minced
>
>½ cup soy sauce
>
>3 tablespoons Asian sesame oil

3 tablespoons sugar

2 teaspoons minced peeled fresh gingerroot

2 teaspoons distilled vinegar

2 teaspoons sesame seeds

1 teaspoon freshly ground black pepper

18 scallions, trimmed

Cut through meaty side of each short rib to bone at ½-inch intervals, leaving meat attached to bone. In a bowl whisk together remaining ingredients except scallions until combined well. Coat each rib thoroughly with marinade, transferring to a large sealable plastic bag. Add scallions and any remaining marinade to bag and seal bag, pressing out excess air. *Marinate ribs, chilled, turning bag occasionally, overnight.*

Prepare grill.

Remove ribs from marinade, letting excess drip off, and grill ribs, meaty side down, on an oiled rack set 5 to 6 inches over glowing coals 8 minutes. Turn ribs over and grill 6 minutes more for medium-rare. Remove scallions from marinade, discarding it, and grill scallions, turning occasionally, 4 minutes, or until just browned.

Serves 6.

Photo on page 132

ASIAN CUCUMBER RIBBON SALAD

3 seedless cucumbers, halved lengthwise and seeded

⅓ cup seasoned rice vinegar*

¾ teaspoon Asian sesame oil

3 tablespoons sesame seeds, toasted lightly and cooled

1 tablespoon finely grated peeled fresh gingerroot

⅓ cup chopped scallion greens

a pinch sugar if desired

*available at Asian markets and some supermarkets

With a *mandoline* or other manual slicer or a vegetable peeler cut cucumbers lengthwise into thin ribbons.

In a bowl toss cucumber ribbons with remaining ingredients and season with salt and pepper. *Chill salad, covered, until cold, at least 15 minutes and up to 1 hour.*

Serves 6.

Photo above

FRAGRANT SUSHI RICE

===

1 tablespoon vegetable oil

1 cup finely chopped carrot

1 teaspoon finely chopped peeled
    fresh gingerroot

1 garlic clove, minced

1½ cups sushi rice* or medium-grain rice

2 cups water

1 teaspoon salt

¼ pound snow peas (about 1 cup),
    trimmed and strings discarded

1 tablespoon sesame seeds, toasted lightly

2 tablespoons seasoned rice vinegar*
    or to taste

*available at Asian markets and some supermarkets

In a large saucepan heat oil over moderately high heat until hot but not smoking and stir-fry carrot until it begins to brown. Add gingerroot and garlic and stir-fry 1 minute. Stir in rice, water, and salt and bring to a boil. Simmer rice, covered, 20 minutes.

While rice is simmering, in a saucepan of boiling water blanch snow peas 15 seconds and transfer with a slotted spoon to a bowl of ice water to stop cooking. Drain snow peas well and slice thin diagonally.

Transfer rice to a large bowl and stir in snow peas, sesame seeds, vinegar, and salt and pepper to taste.

Serves 6.

MIDORI LIME MOUSSES

===

½ cup fresh lime juice (from about 2 limes)

2 tablespoons fresh lemon juice

¼ cup Midori (melon-flavored liqueur)

1 stick (½ cup) unsalted butter, cut into bits

1 cup sugar

2 whole large eggs

2 large egg yolks

1 tablespoon freshly grated lime zest

1 teaspoon unflavored gelatin

1 cup chilled heavy cream

GARNISH: **lime zest strips, tied in knots**

In a small heavy saucepan bring juices and Midori just to a boil and remove pan from heat. Whisk in butter until completely melted. Whisk in sugar, whole eggs, yolks, zest, and gelatin until combined well. Cook custard over moderate heat, whisking constantly, until thickened and it registers 170° F. on a candy thermometer. Pour custard through a fine sieve into a heatproof bowl set over a bowl of ice water and stir until cooled completely.

In a bowl with an electric mixer beat cream until it just holds stiff peaks. Fold cream into custard until just combined and spoon mousse into six dessert glasses. *Chill mousses, loosely covered with plastic wrap, at least 1 hour and up to 24 hours.*

Garnish mousses with lime knots.

Serves 6.

Photo opposite

Pool parties call for refreshing, carefree, easy-to-eat fare. Our "BLTs", made with bacon, fried green tomatoes, and fresh mozzarella, promise to tempt even the most sophisticated appetites. Green tomatoes are usually picked in late summer and early fall, when there is little chance they'll ripen. But they're worth picking or searching out at the farmers market earlier. And, if you can find whimsical racchete (racket-shaped pasta), it's the perfect partner to green pea "tennis balls" in a winning pasta salad. But dessert—our fanciful watermelon sorbet slices—will certainly steal the show. The sorbet is delicious on its own, but if you take the time to assemble the slices and decorate them with chocolate "seeds", you'll make a lasting impression.

◆ Sorbet slices require several steps, but may be made 3 days ahead.

◆ Pasta salad may be made 4 hours ahead.

FRIED GREEN TOMATO, MOZZARELLA, AND BASIL "BLTS"

PROSCIUTTO AND FRESH PEA PASTA SALAD

■

WATERMELON SORBET WITH CHOCOLATE SEEDS

■

Lemonade

SERVES 6

COOL-OFF
POOL PARTY

FRIED GREEN TOMATO, MOZZARELLA, AND BASIL "BLTs"

1 pound sliced bacon

3 pounds green tomatoes (about 6 medium),
    cut into ¼-inch-thick slices

about ⅔ cup yellow cornmeal

12 large slices firm white sandwich bread

1 pound fresh mozzarella, cut into
    ¼-inch-thick slices

about 36 fresh basil leaves

In 10- to 12-inch heavy skillet cook bacon in batches over moderate heat until crisp, reserving ½ cup drippings and transferring bacon to paper towels to drain.

In a bowl coat 4 tomato slices evenly with cornmeal and season with salt. In skillet heat ¼ cup reserved bacon drippings over moderate heat until hot but not smoking and fry tomatoes until golden brown on both sides, about 5 minutes, transferring to paper towels to drain. Coat and fry remaining tomatoes in same manner, using additional drippings if necessary.

Preheat broiler.

On a baking sheet broil one side of bread slices about 3 inches from heat until golden. Make sandwiches by layering, on untoasted sides of 6 bread slices, mozzarella, basil, tomatoes, and bacon. Top with remaining bread slices, toasted sides up.

Makes 6 sandwiches.

PROSCIUTTO AND FRESH PEA PASTA SALAD

¾ pound racchette (racket-shaped pasta),
    or cavatelli or other short pasta

3 tablespoons white-wine vinegar, or to taste

⅓ cup extra-virgin olive oil

1 cup shelled fresh or frozen peas

2½ ounces thinly sliced prosciutto,
    chopped fine (about ½ cup)

½ cup chopped yellow or red bell pepper

½ large sweet onion, sliced thin

¼ cup chopped drained peperoncini
    (pickled Tuscan peppers)

⅓ cup finely chopped assorted fresh herbs
    such as basil, parsley, oregano, and chives

In a kettle bring salted water to a boil for pasta.

In a large bowl whisk together vinegar and salt and pepper to taste and add olive oil in a stream, whisking until combined well.

Cook pasta in boiling water 8 minutes. Add peas and boil until pasta is tender, about 3 minutes more. In a large colander drain pasta and peas and rinse well under cold water. Drain pasta well and add to vinaigrette. Add remaining ingredients and toss well. *Pasta salad may be made 4 hours ahead and chilled, covered.*

Serves 6.

WATERMELON SORBET WITH CHOCOLATE SEEDS

———

a 3½- to 4-pound piece of watermelon (about a quarter of a large watermelon that has been halved lengthwise and crosswise)

1 cup sugar

¼ cup fresh lime juice

2 tablespoons Sambuca or other anise-flavored liqueur if desired

1½ ounces fine-quality bittersweet chocolate (not unsweetened), chopped

Cut watermelon into 6 semicircular slices, each about ¾ inch thick. Cut flesh from rind and chop flesh coarse, reserving rind. Arrange rinds on their sides on 2 foil-lined baking sheets and cover tightly with plastic wrap. *Freeze rinds until frozen hard, about 2 hours.*

Discard real seeds from watermelon flesh. In a blender purée enough flesh to yield 5 cups, transferring it to a large metal bowl. In a saucepan heat 1 cup purée with sugar over moderate heat, stirring, until sugar is dissolved and stir into remaining purée with lime juice and liqueur. *Chill mixture, covered, until cold, about 1 hour.*

Line another baking sheet or a tray with parchment or wax paper. In a small bowl set over a small saucepan of barely simmering water melt chocolate and remove bowl from heat. Transfer chocolate to a small sealable plastic bag and seal bag. Snip off tip of one corner of bag to form a tiny hole and onto baking sheet pipe and spread chocolate into ⅓- by ½-inch ovals to resemble watermelon seeds. *Freeze chocolate "seeds" on baking sheet until very firm, about 30 minutes.* Working quickly, peel "seeds" from paper into another small bowl and keep frozen.

Freeze watermelon mixture in an ice-cream maker. When sorbet is frozen to a thick slush add three fourths of chocolate "seeds" and continue to freeze until frozen.

Working quickly, fill frozen watermelon rinds with sorbet, smoothing it with a spatula, and arrange remaining chocolate "seeds" realistically on slices. Smooth sorbet again. *Freeze slices, covered with plastic wrap, until very firm, at least 6 hours and up to 3 days.*

Makes 6 slices, serving 6.

Photo on page 138

Mid-summer's bounty calls for a celebration, so head out to the farmers market with a copy of our menu in hand. The best time to shop is early morning when you have the pick of the market and produce is at its peak. Our recipes are flexible, so choose whatever looks freshest and best. You may want to try white or variegated eggplant for our rolls, or an heirloom tomato in the vegetable ragout for the cod. And, of course, if the peaches or blackberries look better than the strawberries, buy them instead—our sour cream topping is fabulous on any fruit mixture. Since many farmers markets also offer cheeses, fish, and home-baked bread for sale, you should be able to find almost everything you need.

◆ For eggplant rolls: Salsa verde may be made 1 day ahead; eggplant may be broiled 3 hours ahead; rolls may be assembled 2 hours ahead.

A FARMERS MARKET FEAST

FETA-STUFFED EGGPLANT ROLLS

==

a firm 1-pound eggplant
olive oil for brushing eggplant
3 ounces feta, crumbled (about ½ cup)
⅓ cup whole-milk ricotta
¼ cup fresh mint leaves, chopped fine
3 red bell peppers, roasted (page 116)
1 bunch arugula, coarse stems discarded

ACCOMPANIMENT: *salsa verde (recipe follows)*

Preheat broiler and oil a baking sheet.

Cut eggplant lengthwise into ¼-inch-thick slices and arrange 6 center slices on baking sheet in one layer, reserving remaining eggplant for another use. Brush eggplant with oil and season with salt.

Broil eggplant about 3 inches from heat until golden, about 5 minutes. Carefully turn eggplant over with a metal spatula and broil until top is golden, about 4 minutes more. Transfer eggplant to a platter large enough to hold slices in one layer and cool.

In a small bowl with a fork mash together feta, ricotta, mint, and salt and pepper to taste. Cut peppers lengthwise into pieces about same width as eggplant slices.

Assemble rolls:

Top eggplant slices with pepper pieces, arranging them in one layer. Put 1 tablespoon cheese mixture near narrow end of each slice and onto it gently press 4 or 5 arugula leaves

so that they stick out on both sides. Beginning with cheese end, roll up each slice to enclose cheese mixture and leaves. *Rolls may be made 2 hours ahead and kept, covered loosely, at room temperature.*

Serve rolls drizzled with *salsa verde.*

Serves 6 as a first course.

Photo on page 142

SALSA VERDE

 ==

1 cup packed fresh parsley leaves
1 small garlic clove
⅓ cup extra-virgin olive oil
1 tablespoon red-wine vinegar
½ teaspoon anchovy paste

In a blender purée salsa ingredients until *smooth. Salsa may be made 1 day ahead and chilled, covered. Bring salsa to room temperature before serving.*

Makes about 1 cup.

COD FILLET WITH ROASTED VEGETABLE RAGOUT

==

six 6-ounce pieces skinless cod fillet

3 medium zucchini (about 2¼ pounds total), cut into 1¼-inch pieces

7 plum tomatoes (about 1 pound total), halved

2 large red onions, cut into ½-inch wedges

1½ large yellow bell peppers, cut into ½-inch-wide strips

2 large garlic cloves, crushed

4 fresh thyme sprigs

2 teaspoons vegetable oil

⅓ cup fresh bread crumbs

2 tablespoons chopped fresh flat-leafed parsley leaves

3 tablespoons water

1½ tablespoons soy sauce

1½ tablespoons fresh lemon juice

1 tablespoon Worcestershire sauce

Preheat oven to 500° F.

Season cod with salt and pepper. In a large shallow baking pan toss zucchini, tomatoes, onions, bell peppers, garlic, and thyme with oil and salt and pepper to taste and spread in one layer. Roast vegetables in middle of oven 20 minutes, or until they begin to brown. Arrange fish over vegetables and roast 7 minutes, or until just cooked through.

While fish is roasting, in a small skillet toast bread crumbs with parsley and salt and pepper to taste over moderate heat, stirring, until golden, about 5 minutes.

Transfer fish carefully to a plate and keep warm, covered. To vegetables add water, soy sauce, lemon juice, and Worcestershire sauce and stir to loosen brown bits from bottom of pan and break up tomatoes.

Serve ragout topped with fish and bread crumbs.

Serves 6.

Photo opposite

STRAWBERRIES WITH BROWN SUGAR SOUR CREAM

 ==

1½ cups sour cream

2 tablespoons packed light brown sugar

½ teaspoon vanilla

1½ quarts strawberries, hulled and halved

In a small bowl stir together sour cream, brown sugar, and vanilla. Divide berries among 6 dessert dishes and top with a dollop of brown sugar sour cream.

Serves 6.

GAZPACHO

———

FLANK STEAK FAJITAS

BLACK BEAN SALSA

YELLOW RICE SALAD

———

ANGEL FOOD CAKE WITH
CINNAMON PLUM SAUCE

———

Quivira Dry Creek Zinfandel 1994

SERVES 6

Hot summer days call for dishes that can be prepared ahead of time during the coolest hours of the day (either the night before or that morning), then served chilled or at room temperature. Our Southwestern-inspired repast fits the bill, requiring only last-minute grilling of the steak and tortillas for fajitas. Fresh flour tortillas make all the difference—try the Maria and Ricardo's Tortilla Factory brand. To avoid heating up your oven, buy an angel food cake and top it with our luscious plum sauce.

◆ Steak for fajitas must marinate at least 12 hours and up to 24.

◆ Gazpacho must be chilled at least 4 hours or overnight.

◆ Salsa must be chilled at least 2 hours.

◆ Plum sauce for dessert must be chilled at least 2 hours and up to 24.

◆ Rice salad may be made 2 hours ahead.

REPAST IN THE SHADE

Gazpacho

2½ pounds vine-ripened tomatoes (about
    5 large), peeled and seeded (procedure
    follows) and chopped fine

½ pound seedless cucumber, cut into
    ½-inch cubes

1 cup finely chopped red onion

1 red bell pepper, chopped fine

1 yellow bell pepper, chopped fine

¾ teaspoon minced garlic

¼ cup extra-virgin olive oil

¼ cup red-wine vinegar

1 cup bottled or canned tomato juice

1 cup beef broth

1 tablespoon tomato paste

1 teaspoon ground cumin

1 teaspoon salt

1 tablespoon Worcestershire sauce

½ cup ice cubes

GARNISH: **thin cucumber slices and julienne
    strips of red and yellow bell pepper**

In a bowl stir together all ingredients except ice cubes until combined well and season with black pepper. Stir in ice cubes. *Chill soup, covered, at least 4 hours or overnight.*

    Serve soup in chilled bowls and garnish with cucumber slices and bell pepper strips.

    Makes about 8 cups, serving 6.

Photo on page 146

To Peel and Seed Tomatoes

With a sharp knife cut a small X in bottom end of tomatoes. In a kettle of boiling salted water blanch tomatoes 10 seconds, or until skin starts to curl at X. Transfer tomatoes with a slotted spoon to a bowl of ice water and let stand until cool enough to handle. Remove skin. Halve tomatoes crosswise and with a small spoon scoop out seeds.

Flank Steak Fajitas

FOR MARINADE

    ¼ **cup dry red wine**

    3 **tablespoons fresh lemon juice**

    3 **tablespoons vegetable oil**

    3 **garlic cloves, minced and mashed to a paste
        with 1 teaspoon salt**

    ½ **teaspoon dried hot red pepper flakes, or to
        taste**

    1½ **pounds flank steak**

ACCOMPANIMENTS:

    2 **avocados (preferably California), chopped
        and tossed with 2 teaspoons fresh
        lemon juice**

    4 **cups shredded romaine or iceberg lettuce**

    black bean salsa (page 150)

    1 **cup sour cream**

    twelve 7- to 8-inch flour tortillas*

    *available at most supermarkets and by mail order
      (page 231)*

Make marinade:

In a shallow bowl stir together marinade ingredients and transfer to a large sealable plastic bag.

Add steak to marinade, turning to coat, and seal bag, pressing out excess air. *Marinate steak, chilled, at least 12 hours and up to 24.*

Prepare grill.

Remove steak from marinade, letting excess drip off, and discard marinade. Grill steak on an oiled rack set 5 to 6 inches over glowing coals 5 to 6 minutes on each side for medium-rare. Transfer steak to a cutting board and let stand 10 minutes.

While steak is standing, on coolest part of grill briefly warm tortillas until heated through but still pliable, about 30 seconds on each side.

Slice steak thin across grain on the diagonal and serve with avocado, lettuce, salsa, sour cream, and tortillas for wrapping.

Serves 6.

BLACK BEAN SALSA

==

3 cups canned black beans (about two
     15-ounce cans), drained and rinsed

1½ cups chopped seeded vine-ripened
     tomatoes (about 2 large)

1 cup chopped yellow or red bell pepper

½ cup chopped red onion

2 or 3 jalapeño or serrano chilies, or to taste
     (include some seeds for hotter salsa),
     seeded and chopped (wear rubber gloves)

¼ cup packed fresh coriander sprigs,
     chopped coarse

½ teaspoon ground cumin

3 tablespoons fresh lime juice

2 tablespoons vegetable oil

½ teaspoon salt

In a bowl toss together all ingredients until
combined well. *Chill salsa, covered, at least 2
hours and up to 24.*

Serves 6.

YELLOW RICE SALAD

 ==

¼ cup olive oil

2 teaspoons cumin seeds

2 cups long-grain white rice

4 cups water

½ teaspoon turmeric

¾ teaspoon salt

1 cup sliced California black olives

1 cup cooked fresh or thawed frozen corn

½ cup pine nuts, toasted golden

½ cup thinly sliced scallion

3 tablespoons white-wine vinegar

In a 3-quart heavy saucepan heat 1 tablespoon oil over moderately high heat until hot
but not smoking and sauté cumin seeds, stirring, 10 seconds, or until fragrant and a few
shades darker. Add rice and sauté, stirring, 1
to 2 minutes, or until rice is well coated. Stir
in water, turmeric, and salt and boil, uncovered, without stirring, 6 to 8 minutes, or until
surface is covered with steam holes and grains
on top appear dry. Reduce heat as much as
possible and cook rice, covered, 10 minutes
more. Remove pan from heat and let rice
stand, covered, 5 minutes.

Transfer rice to a bowl and add olives,
corn, pine nuts, scallion, vinegar, remaining 3
tablespoons oil, and salt and pepper to taste,
tossing to combine well. *Salad may be made 2
hours ahead and kept, partially covered, at
room temperature.*

Serves 6.

Angel Food Cake with Cinnamon Plum Sauce

½ cup water

½ cup sugar

1 pound plums (about 5), pitted
    and cut into eighths

1 teaspoon freshly grated lime zest

1 teaspoon vanilla

¼ teaspoon cinnamon

a pinch ground black pepper

1 angel food cake (store-bought)

In a large saucepan bring ½ cup water and sugar to a boil, stirring until sugar is dissolved, and simmer 5 minutes. Add plums and zest and cook at a slow boil, adding additional water if mixture becomes dry, 10 minutes, or until plums are soft and fall apart. In a food processor purée mixture until smooth. Force purée through a fine sieve into a bowl and stir in vanilla, cinnamon, pepper, and a pinch salt. Cool sauce. *Chill sauce, covered, at least 2 hours and up to 1 day.*

Slice angel food cake and serve with sauce.

Makes about 2 cups sauce.

Photo below

From bubbly Kir spritzers to a fresh blueberry tart, this summer luncheon boasts special touches —endive spears for dipping in the yogurt tahini, fresh currants to garnish the lamb, and three miniature tomato varieties (pear, cherry, and whole currant) for the salad. Naturally, if availability is a problem, feel free to make substitutions—but never ordinary ones. Crisp cucumber or zucchini spears make great-looking crudités, a chiffonade (thin strips) of fresh mint is a lovely embellishment for the meat, and any mix of vine-ripened tomatoes, yellow varieties included, will do nicely in the salad.

♦ Tabbouleh may be made 1 day ahead.

♦ Tart must be chilled about 4 hours and up to 1 day.

♦ Yogurt tahini dip may be made 2 hours ahead.

KIR SPRITZERS

YOGURT TAHINI DIP WITH CRUDITÉS AND PITA

■

GRILLED LEG OF LAMB WITH RED CURRANT SAUCE

HERBED TABBOULEH

SUMMER TOMATO SALAD

■

BLUEBERRY TART

■

Château Musar Lebanese Red Wine 1989

SERVES 8

SUNDAY LUNCH
ON THE VERANDA

KIR SPRITZER

¼ cup dry white wine

1 tablespoon Chambord (black-raspberry-
flavored liqueur) or crème de cassis, or
to taste

fresh seltzer or club soda, chilled

GARNISH: 1 strip fresh lemon zest

In a stemmed glass half filled with ice cubes
combine wine and liqueur. Top off drink with
seltzer or club soda.

Garnish drink with zest.

Makes 1 drink.

YOGURT TAHINI DIP WITH CRUDITÉS AND PITA

1 cup plain yogurt

3 tablespoons well-stirred tahini
(sesame seed paste)

2 tablespoons extra-virgin olive oil

3 garlic cloves, minced and mashed
to a paste with ½ teaspoon salt

2 teaspoons fresh oregano leaves,
chopped fine

¼ teaspoon ground cumin

⅛ teaspoon cayenne

½ cup finely chopped peeled
seeded cucumber

ACCOMPANIMENTS:

3 Belgian endives, separated into leaves

4 carrots, cut into sticks

4 pita loaves, cut into wedges

In a bowl whisk together yogurt, *tahini*, oil,
garlic, oregano, cumin, and cayenne and stir
in cucumber until combined well. *Dip may be
made 2 hours ahead and chilled, covered.*

Serve dip with crudités and pita wedges.

Makes about 1½ cups dip.

GRILLED LEG OF LAMB WITH RED CURRANT SAUCE

1½ teaspoons coarse salt

1½ teaspoons coarsely ground black pepper

1¼ teaspoons ground coriander seed

¼ teaspoon cinnamon

a 7- to 8-pound leg of lamb, trimmed of excess
fat, boned, and butterflied by butcher
(4 to 4¾ pounds boneless)

FOR SAUCE

1 tablespoon red currant jelly

¼ cup fresh lemon juice

¼ cup olive oil

½ teaspoon ground cumin

GARNISH: romaine or Bibb lettuce leaves and
2 cups fresh currants

Prepare grill or preheat broiler.

In a small bowl stir together salt, pepper, coriander, and cinnamon and rub all over lamb. Grill lamb on an oiled rack set 5 to 6 inches over glowing coals 7 to 10 minutes on each side, or until a meat thermometer inserted in thickest part registers 140° F. for medium-rare. (Alternatively, lamb may be broiled under broiler about 4 inches from heat.) Transfer lamb to a cutting board and let stand 10 minutes.

Make sauce:

In a small saucepan heat jelly over moderately low heat, stirring until melted. Remove pan from heat and into jelly whisk remaining sauce ingredients and salt and pepper to taste.

Slice lamb thin across the grain and arrange on a platter lined with lettuce. Drizzle lamb with sauce and garnish with currants.

Serves 8.

SUMMER TOMATO SALAD

⅓ cup vegetable oil

3 tablespoons Champagne vinegar or white-wine vinegar, or to taste

a 2- by ½-inch strip lemon zest removed with a vegetable peeler and cut lengthwise into fine julienne

¼ cup chopped fresh chives

2 teaspoons fresh thyme leaves

¼ teaspoon sugar

3 pounds pear tomatoes and cherry tomatoes, halved, and whole currant tomatoes

In a large bowl whisk together all ingredients except tomatoes and season with salt and pepper. Add tomatoes and toss gently. Let salad stand at room temperature 30 minutes before serving.

Serves 8.

HERBED TABBOULEH

=

2 cups water

1 cup bulgur

8 cups packed fresh parsley leaves
(about 4 large bunches)

1 cup packed fresh mint leaves

1 cup packed fresh coriander sprigs

½ cup thinly sliced scallion

¼ cup olive oil

¼ cup fresh lemon juice

In a small saucepan bring water to a boil. Remove pan from heat and stir in bulgur. *Soak bulgur 1 hour.*

Chop herbs fine. Drain bulgur in a fine sieve, pressing hard to extract as much water as possible. In a large bowl toss together bulgur, herbs, remaining ingredients, and salt and pepper to taste until combined well. *Tabbouleh may be made 1 day ahead and chilled, covered.*

Serves 8.

BLUEBERRY TART

===

FOR CRUST

> 1¼ cups all-purpose flour
>
> ¼ cup sugar
>
> ¼ teaspoon salt
>
> 1 stick (½ cup) cold unsalted butter, cut into bits
>
> 1 large egg yolk

FOR FILLING

> a ¼-ounce envelope unflavored gelatin (about 2½ teaspoons)
>
> 3 tablespoons water
>
> 1 tablespoon fresh lemon juice
>
> ½ cup sugar
>
> ¼ teaspoon cinnamon
>
> 8 cups picked-over blueberries
>
> 1 tablespoon vanilla
>
> ACCOMPANIMENT: whipped cream

Make crust:

Preheat oven to 400° F.

In a food processor blend together flour, sugar, salt, and butter until mixture resembles meal. Add yolk and pulse until dough begins to come together but is still crumbly.

Press dough evenly onto bottom and up side of an 11-inch tart pan with a removable fluted rim. Prick bottom of crust all over with a fork and chill 30 minutes.

Bake crust in middle of oven 20 to 25 minutes, or until golden, and cool in pan on a rack.

Make filling:

In a small bowl sprinkle gelatin over water to soften. In a saucepan simmer lemon juice, sugar, cinnamon, a pinch salt, and 3 cups blueberries, stirring occasionally, 10 minutes. Remove pan from heat and into berry mixture stir gelatin mixture and vanilla until gelatin is dissolved. Transfer mixture to a metal bowl set in a larger bowl of ice water and stir until thickened to the consistency of raw egg white but not set, about 15 minutes. Fold in remaining 5 cups berries and pour filling into crust, spreading evenly. *Chill tart, loosely covered, at least until set, about 4 hours and up to 1 day.*

Serve tart with whipped cream.

Photo on page 152

If you'd prefer, this robust Italian feast also could be served as a relaxed alfresco lunch or supper. Find a shaded area by the water for your buffet table, and put out all the platters (except dessert) at once to allow everyone to help themselves. Later in the day, bring out the berries and the biscotti with a pot of espresso or strong coffee.

◆ Biscotti may be made 3 days ahead.

◆ Frittatas may be made 1 hour ahead if serving warm; 1 day ahead if serving at room temperature.

◆ Pasta salad may be made 1 day ahead.

◆ Cauliflower salad must marinate at least 1 hour and up to 1 day.

MELON WITH PROSCIUTTO

OLIVES, CHEESES, FIGS, AND MIXED GREENS

SAUSAGE AND ESCAROLE FRITTATA

CAULIFLOWER AND ARTICHOKE SALAD

TUNA PASTA SALAD

▬

MIXED BERRIES WITH YOGURT CREAM

ESPRESSO HAZELNUT BISCOTTI

▬

*Sanford Santa Barbara County
Pinot Noir Vin Gris 1995*

SERVES 8

WATERSIDE ANTIPASTO BRUNCH

MELON WITH PROSCIUTTO

sixteen ½-inch-thick wedges peeled
   cantaloupe (about 1½ melons)
16 thin slices prosciutto (about ½
   to ⅔ pound)
fresh lemon juice for sprinkling
   on melon
olive oil for drizzling on prosciutto
   if desired
a ¼-pound piece Parmesan, at room
   temperature
freshly ground black pepper

GARNISH: *lemon slices*

On a platter arrange melon and prosciutto
separately. Sprinkle melon with lemon juice
and drizzle prosciutto with oil. With a vegetable peeler shave Parmesan into curls over
prosciutto and season melon and prosciutto
with pepper.

Garnish platter with lemon slices.

Serves 8.

Photo on page 158

OLIVES, CHEESES, FIGS, AND MIXED GREENS

FOR VINAIGRETTE

6 tablespoons red-wine vinegar
¼ cup minced shallot
1 teaspoon Dijon mustard
two 2- by ½-inch strips orange zest, removed
   with a vegetable peeler and cut
   lengthwise into fine julienne strips
⅔ cup extra-virgin olive oil

¾ pound assorted brine-cured olives
a ½-pound piece Gorgonzola
a ½-pound piece Italian Fontina (preferably
   Val d'Aosta)
a ½-pound piece Parmesan
¾ pound fresh figs, halved
10 cups mixed salad greens (about ½ pound)

ACCOMPANIMENT: *2 round crusty bread loaves*

Make vinaigrette:

In a small bowl whisk together vinegar,
shallot, mustard, zest, and salt and pepper to
taste and add oil in a stream, whisking until
combined well.

In a small bowl toss olives with about 1
tablespoon vinaigrette. Arrange cheeses and
figs on a small platter. Put greens in a large
bowl. Season greens with salt and pepper and
drizzle with 3 tablespoons vinaigrette.

Serve olives, cheeses, figs, and greens with
bread and remaining vinaigrette on the side.

Serves 8 generously.

SAUSAGE AND ESCAROLE FRITTATA

==

4 sweet or hot fresh Italian sausages

4 teaspoons olive oil

1 small red bell pepper, chopped

1 medium zucchini, chopped

¾ pound escarole, chopped fine

8 large eggs

4 teaspoons fresh tarragon leaves, chopped

In a dry large non-stick skillet cook sausages over moderately low heat, turning occasionally, 20 minutes, or until cooked through, and transfer to a cutting board. Cool sausages slightly and cut into ¼-inch pieces.

Pour off fat from skillet. In skillet heat 1 teaspoon oil over moderately high heat until hot but not smoking and sauté bell pepper and zucchini, stirring, until softened. Add 1 teaspoon oil and escarole and sauté, stirring, until escarole is tender, about 5 minutes. Stir in sausage and season with salt and pepper. Remove pan from heat and cool mixture slightly.

Preheat broiler and lightly oil a large baking sheet.

In a large bowl lightly beat eggs and stir in sausage mixture, tarragon, and salt and pepper to taste. In a flameproof 10-inch non-stick skillet heat 1 teaspoon oil over moderately low heat until hot but not smoking and add half of egg mixture, tilting skillet to distribute evenly. Cook egg mixture until set underneath but still slightly wet in center, 3 to 4 minutes.

Broil frittata 4 to 5 inches from heat until set and top is golden brown, 2 to 3 minutes. Slide frittata out of skillet (keep right side up) onto baking sheet and keep warm, covered with foil. Make another frittata with remaining teaspoon oil and egg mixture in same manner. *Frittatas may be made 1 hour ahead and kept warm, covered with foil, in a 225° F. oven. (Alternatively, frittatas may be made 1 day ahead and cooled completely before being chilled, covered. Allow frittatas to return to room temperature before serving.)*

Serve frittatas warm or at room temperature, cut into wedges.

Makes 2 frittatas, serving 8.

CAULIFLOWER AND ARTICHOKE SALAD

==

1 pound fresh fava beans, shelled
    (about 1 cup)

½ head cauliflower, cut into flowerets

¼ cup chopped onion

4 garlic cloves, minced

⅓ cup extra-virgin olive oil

¼ cup fresh lemon juice

¼ cup chopped flat-leafed parsley leaves

2 teaspoons dried oregano, crumbled

1 teaspoon fennel seeds, crushed lightly

¼ teaspoon dried hot red pepper flakes

¾ teaspoon salt

½ teaspoon black pepper

two 14-ounce cans artichoke hearts, rinsed,
    drained, and quartered

1 bay leaf

In a kettle of salted boiling water blanch beans 10 seconds and transfer with a slotted spoon to a bowl of ice water. Drain beans and gently peel away outer skins. To kettle add cauliflower and boil 5 minutes. Drain cauliflower well and transfer to another bowl of ice water to stop cooking. Drain cauliflower well.

In a bowl whisk together onion, garlic, oil, juice, parsley, oregano, fennel seeds, pepper flakes, salt, and black pepper until combined well. Add beans, cauliflower, artichokes, and bay leaf and toss until combined well. *Marinate salad at least 1 hour at room temperature or up to 1 day, covered and chilled.*

Serves 8.

TUNA PASTA SALAD

1 pound medium pasta shells

⅓ cup sun-dried tomatoes (not packed in oil)

1 medium onion, chopped

2 garlic cloves, minced

⅓ cup extra-virgin olive oil plus 1 tablespoon
    additional if necessary

a 6- to 7½-ounce can tuna packed in olive oil,
    drained and flaked

2 flat anchovy fillets, chopped fine

¼ cup chopped flat-leafed parsley leaves

1 medium vine-ripened tomato, chopped

1 tablespoon balsamic vinegar plus
    1 tablespoon additional if necessary

Bring a kettle of salted water to a boil for pasta shells.

In a heatproof bowl soak sun-dried tomatoes in 1 cup boiling water 5 minutes. Drain tomatoes in a sieve set over a bowl, reserving ¼ cup liquid. Chop soaked tomatoes.

Cook pasta in boiling water until *al dente.*

While pasta is cooking, in a heavy skillet cook onion and garlic in ⅓ cup oil over moderate heat, stirring, until pale golden. Add soaked tomatoes, tuna, anchovies, parsley, reserved soaking liquid, and salt and pepper to taste and simmer 1 minute.

Drain pasta well and in a bowl toss with tuna mixture, tomato, 1 tablespoon vinegar, and salt and pepper to taste. *Salad may be made 1 day ahead and chilled, covered. Return to room temperature and toss with additional vinegar and oil and salt and pepper to taste.*

Serves 8.

ESPRESSO HAZELNUT BISCOTTI

═

2½ cups unbleached all-purpose flour

1 cup packed light brown sugar

3 tablespoons instant espresso powder

1 teaspoon finely grated fresh lemon zest

½ teaspoon baking soda

½ teaspoon baking powder

½ teaspoon salt

3 large eggs

1 teaspoon vanilla

1 cup whole hazelnuts

an egg wash made by beating together 1 large egg and 1 teaspoon water

Preheat oven to 325° F. and butter and flour 2 large baking sheets, knocking out excess flour.

In bowl of a standing electric mixer fitted with paddle attachment beat together flour, brown sugar, espresso powder, zest, baking soda, baking powder, and salt until combined well and beat in eggs and vanilla just until a dough forms. Stir in hazelnuts.

On a lightly floured surface knead dough several times. Halve dough and with floured hands form each half into a flattish log, 13 inches long and 1 inch wide. Put both logs at least 4 inches apart on one baking sheet and brush with egg wash.

Bake logs in middle of oven 30 minutes. Cool logs on baking sheet on a rack 10 minutes. On a cutting board cut logs crosswise on the diagonal into ¾-inch-thick slices and arrange *biscotti*, cut sides down, on two baking sheets. Bake *biscotti* in upper and lower thirds of oven 8 minutes. Remove sheets from oven and turn *biscotti* over with a spatula. Return *biscotti* to oven, switching position of sheets, and bake 8 minutes more, or until *biscotti* are slightly darker. Transfer *biscotti* to racks and cool. *Biscotti keep 3 days in an airtight container at room temperature.*

Makes about 30 biscotti.

MIXED BERRIES WITH YOGURT CREAM

 ═

1 quart strawberries, hulled and if large halved

4 cups mixed berries such as wild blueberries, raspberries, and blackberries

2 tablespoons Grand Marnier or other orange-flavored liqueur

2 tablespoons sugar

2 teaspoons balsamic vinegar

8 ounces vanilla yogurt

½ teaspoon vanilla

¼ cup heavy cream

In a large bowl toss berries with liqueur, sugar, and vinegar. Macerate berries 15 minutes and toss again.

In a bowl whisk together yogurt and vanilla. In a bowl with an electric mixer beat cream just until it holds stiff peaks and fold into yogurt mixture.

Serve berries topped with yogurt cream.

Serves 8.

Kids can be finicky, so on their day why not serve "safe" old-fashioned favorites (with a bit of flair) that will please both young guests and their parents. Just for fun, we used rotelle (wagon wheel) pasta for the baked macaroni and cheese; made our own pigs-in-blankets with parent-friendly wheat-germ and buttermilk; and added apple and honey to the coleslaw for sweetness and color. Instead of a traditional cake, we offer cupcakes that everyone gets to frost themselves (that is, if mom says it's okay) with orange, chocolate, or butterscotch frosting.

◆ Ranch dip may be made 1 day ahead.

◆ Frosted cupcakes may be made 1 day ahead.

◆ Pigs-in-blankets may be prepared, up to baking, 1 day ahead.

◆ Macaroni and cheese may be prepared, in part, 1 day ahead.

PIGS-IN-BLANKETS

BAKED MACARONI AND CHEESE

COLESLAW

VEGETABLE STICKS WITH RANCH DIP

■

VANILLA AND CHOCOLATE CUPCAKES
WITH THREE FROSTINGS

■

assorted fruit juices and milk

SERVES 8

BIRTHDAY PARTY
FOR THE KIDS

PIGS-IN-BLANKETS

=

1 cup all-purpose flour

1 teaspoon baking powder

¼ teaspoon baking soda

¼ teaspoon salt

3 tablespoons toasted wheat germ

¼ cup cold vegetable shortening

⅓ cup buttermilk or plain yogurt

1 large egg yolk

10 frankfurters, halved crosswise and ends trimmed

Preheat oven to 375° F. and grease a large baking sheet.

In a bowl whisk together flour, baking powder, baking soda, salt, and wheat germ. With a pastry blender or your fingertips blend in shortening until mixture resembles coarse meal. In a small bowl whisk together buttermilk or yogurt and yolk and stir into flour mixture until mixture just forms a moist dough.

On a floured surface knead dough 4 times and with a floured rolling pin roll out into a 12-inch square. Cut dough into 1½-inch-wide strips and roll a strip around middle of a frankfurter piece just until dough overlaps, cutting pig-in-blanket free from strip. Make 19 more pigs-in-blankets in same manner, arranging each, seam side down, on baking sheet. *Pigs-in-blankets may be prepared up to this point 1 day ahead and chilled, covered.*

Bake pigs-in-blankets in upper third of oven until pale golden, about 15 minutes.

Makes 20 pigs-in-blankets.

Photo on page 164

BAKED MACARONI AND CHEESE

=

¾ pound rotelle (wagon-wheel pasta)

3 tablespoons unsalted butter

3½ tablespoons all-purpose flour

½ teaspoon paprika

3 cups milk

1 teaspoon salt

1 tablespoon Worcestershire sauce

10 ounces Cheddar, grated coarse (about 2¾ cups)

1 cup coarse fresh bread crumbs

Preheat oven to 375° F. and butter a 2-quart shallow baking dish.

Bring a kettle of salted water to a boil for *rotelle*.

In a heavy saucepan melt butter over moderately low heat and whisk in flour and paprika. Cook *roux*, whisking, 3 minutes and whisk in milk and salt. Bring sauce to a boil, whisking, and simmer, whisking occasionally, 3 minutes. Remove pan from heat.

Stir *rotelle* into kettle of boiling water and cook until *al dente*. Drain pasta in a colander and in a large bowl stir together pasta, sauce, Worcestershire sauce, and 2 cups Cheddar. Transfer mixture to baking dish. *Macaroni and cheese may be prepared up to this point 1 day ahead and chilled, covered tightly.*

In a small bowl toss remaining Cheddar with bread crumbs and sprinkle over pasta mixture. Bake macaroni and cheese in middle of oven 25 to 30 minutes, or until golden and bubbling, and let stand 10 minutes before serving.

Serves 8 children.

Photo on page 164

COLESLAW

FOR DRESSING

½ cup mayonnaise

1 tablespoon honey

2 teaspoons cider vinegar

½ teaspoon salt

1 Granny Smith apple

½ medium head green cabbage, halved lengthwise and sliced very thin (about 4 cups)

½ medium head red cabbage, halved lengthwise and sliced very thin (about 4 cups)

2 carrots, shredded fine

Make dressing:

In a large bowl whisk together dressing ingredients.

Coarsely shred apple and add to dressing with cabbages and carrots. Toss coleslaw well.

Serves 8 children.

Photo on page 164

VEGETABLE STICKS WITH RANCH DIP

5 ounces cream cheese

¼ cup buttermilk

2 tablespoons mayonnaise

1 tablespoon grated onion

1 small garlic clove, minced and mashed to a paste with ¼ teaspoon salt

2 teaspoons fresh lemon juice

1 teaspoon sugar

carrots, celery, cucumbers, and/or red bell peppers, cut into sticks

In a blender blend together all ingredients except vegetable sticks and add salt and pepper to taste, blending until smooth. *Dip may be made 1 day ahead and chilled, covered.*

Serve dip with vegetable sticks.

Makes about 1 cup dip.

Vanilla and Chocolate Cupcakes with Three Frostings

===

1 cup all-purpose flour

1 teaspoon baking powder

¼ teaspoon baking soda

⅛ teaspoon salt

¾ stick (6 tablespoons) unsalted butter, softened

½ cup sugar

1 large egg

1 teaspoon vanilla

½ cup milk

3 tablespoons unsweetened cocoa powder (not Dutch-process)

three-in-one frosting (recipe follows)

Preheat oven to 350° F. and line twelve ½-cup muffin tins with paper liners.

Into a bowl sift together flour, baking powder, baking soda, and salt. In another bowl with an electric mixer beat together butter and sugar until light and fluffy and beat in egg and vanilla until smooth. Add flour mixture alternately with milk, beating well after each addition. Spoon half of batter into 6 muffin tins, filling each less than half full. Stir cocoa powder into remaining batter and spoon into remaining tins.

Bake cupcakes in middle of oven 15 to 20 minutes, or until a tester comes out clean.

Turn cupcakes out onto a rack and let cool completely. Spread cupcakes with desired frosting. *Frosted cupcakes may be made 1 day ahead and chilled, covered.*

Makes 6 vanilla and 6 chocolate cupcakes.

Photo opposite

Three-In-One-Frosting

 ===

3 ounces cream cheese, softened

½ stick (¼ cup) unsalted butter, softened

3 tablespoons milk

½ teaspoon salt

a 1-pound box confectioners' sugar (about 4 cups)

1 ounce unsweetened chocolate, melted and cooled

½ cup butterscotch chips, melted and cooled

1 teaspoon freshly grated orange zest

In a bowl with an electric mixer beat together cream cheese and butter until smooth. Beat in milk and salt and gradually add confectioners' sugar, beating until smooth. Divide frosting among 3 bowls. Beat melted chocolate into first bowl to make chocolate frosting. With cleaned beaters beat melted butterscotch chips into second bowl to make butterscotch frosting. With cleaned beaters beat zest into third bowl to make orange frosting.

Makes 3 frostings, enough to frost 12 cupcakes generously.

A Florida vacation may come to mind as you enjoy the tropical, Southern flavors of our chic party. Blender drinks can be frothed up in seconds if you prepare the juices, fruit, and garnishes ahead. Be sure to have extras of each on hand so that you can make new batches as needed. If you cannot find the stone crab claws, jumbo shrimp are a good alternative. All the hors d'oeuvres can be made, at least in part, before your guests arrive.

ORANGE AND APRICOT RUM FIZZES

FROZEN MANGORITAS

MINTY LEMON COOLERS

FRESH HERB PIZZETTA

CURRIED ORANGE PITA CRISPS

ROASTED SWEET POTATO BITES

PULLED PORK ON TORTILLA CHIPS

INDONESIAN PEANUT DIP
WITH CRUDITÉS

STONE CRAB CLAWS
WITH PARSLEY SAUCE

SERVES 16 TO 20

◆ Pita crisps may be made 5 days ahead.

◆ Pulled pork for tortilla chips may be prepared 2 days ahead.

◆ Orange mixture for the rum fizzes may be made 1 day ahead.

◆ Indonesian dip may be made 1 day ahead.

◆ Sauce for the crab may be made 1 day ahead.

◆ Pizzetta may be made 4 hours ahead.

◆ Sweet potato rounds for potato bites may be roasted 2 hours ahead.

COCKTAILS AT FIVE

ORANGE AND APRICOT RUM FIZZES

1½ cups fresh orange juice, chilled
½ cup light rum
¼ cup apricot brandy
2 tablespoons fresh lime juice
fresh club soda or seltzer, chilled

GARNISH: *lime slices*

In a pitcher stir together orange juice, rum, brandy, and lime juice. *Orange mixture may be made 1 day ahead and chilled, covered.* Fill ice-filled tall glasses three-fourths full with orange mixture and top off drinks with club soda or seltzer.

Stir drinks and garnish with lime slices.

Makes 6 drinks.

Photo on page 170

FROZEN MANGORITAS

1 medium mango (about 1 pound),
    peeled and cut into chunks
1 cup white Tequila
½ cup Alizé (passion-fruit-flavored Cognac)
½ cup fresh lime juice
3 tablespoons apricot jam, or to taste

In a blender combine ingredients and enough ice cubes to fill blender and blend just until smooth.

Makes 4 to 6 drinks.

MINTY LEMON COOLERS

2 cups store-bought lemonade
½ cup fresh mint leaves
1¼ cups vodka
1 lemon, sliced
fresh club soda or seltzer, chilled

GARNISH: *fresh mint sprigs*

In a blender blend lemonade and mint leaves until mint is finely chopped. Transfer mixture to a pitcher and stir in vodka and lemon slices. Fill ice-filled tall glasses three-fourths full with vodka mixture and top off drinks with club soda or seltzer.

Stir drinks and garnish with mint.

Makes 6 drinks.

FRESH HERB PIZZETTA

24 small sun-dried tomatoes
     (not packed in oil)
1 frozen puff pastry sheet (half a
     17¼-ounce package), thawed
½ cup bottled olive paste such as tapenade
½ cup finely chopped scallion
2¼ cups finely chopped mixed fresh herbs
     such as basil, mint, dill, and flat-leafed
     parsley (about 3 cups packed leaves)
¼ cup freshly grated Parmesan
2 tablespoons extra-virgin olive oil

In a heatproof bowl soak tomatoes in boiling-hot water to cover 20 minutes, or until softened. Drain tomatoes and pat dry.

Preheat oven to 400° F.

On a lightly floured surface roll out pastry into a 15- by 10-inch rectangle (do not trim edges) and transfer to a large baking sheet. With a fork prick pastry lightly all over.

Spread olive paste evenly over pastry, leaving a ½-inch border all around. Sprinkle olive paste with scallion and 2 cups herbs and arrange tomatoes on top. Sprinkle *pizzetta* with Parmesan and drizzle with oil.

Bake *pizzetta* in middle of oven 15 to 20 minutes, or until golden. Cool *pizzetta* slightly on baking sheet and sprinkle with remaining ¼ cup herbs. *Pizzetta may be made 4 hours ahead and kept at room temperature.*

Cut *pizzetta* into 24 squares and serve warm or at room temperature.

Serves 16 to 20 as an hors d'oeuvre.

Photo above

CURRIED ORANGE PITA CRISPS

zest of 1 navel orange removed with a
     vegetable peeler and chopped
½ cup olive oil
1½ teaspoons curry powder
four 6-inch pita loaves, split
coarse salt for sprinkling pita crisps

Preheat oven to 350° F.

In a blender purée zest with oil and curry powder until smooth and transfer to a small bowl. Brush rough sides of pita halves with curry oil and cut into ¼-inch-wide strips. Divide strips between 2 baking sheets and sprinkle with salt.

Bake pita strips in upper and lower thirds of oven 10 to 12 minutes, or until golden. *Pita crisps keep in an airtight container at room temperature 5 days.*

Serves 16 to 20 as an hors d'oeuvre.

Photo on page 170

ROASTED SWEET POTATO BITES

===

¼ cup vegetable oil

2 large long narrow sweet potatoes
    (about 1½ pounds total), scrubbed
    and left unpeeled

coarse salt for sprinkling potatoes

8 ounces mild goat cheese, softened

1 tablespoon chopped fresh basil leaves

1 teaspoon fresh thyme leaves

1 tablespoon olive oil

three 7-ounce jars whole roasted red peppers,
    drained

about 100 very small fresh basil leaves

Preheat oven to 400° F. and brush a baking sheet with some vegetable oil.

Cut potatoes crosswise into ¼-inch-thick rounds. Arrange rounds in one layer on baking sheet (make sure rounds do not touch) and brush with vegetable oil. Roast rounds in upper third of oven 18 to 22 minutes, or until golden and crisp on bottom. Transfer rounds to paper towels to drain and sprinkle with coarse salt. *Rounds may be roasted 2 hours ahead and cooled completely before being kept, loosely covered, at room temperature.*

Into a small bowl crumble goat cheese and add basil, thyme, olive oil, and freshly ground black pepper to taste, tossing until just combined. Cut roasted peppers into triangles, each just small enough to fit within edge of a potato round. Top potato rounds with pepper triangles and mound ½ teaspoon goat cheese

mixture on each triangle. Tuck 2 basil leaves under each triangle.

Makes about 50 hors d'oeuvres.

Photo on front jacket

PULLED PORK ON TORTILLA CHIPS

===

2½ pounds untrimmed boneless pork shoulder
    or butt, cut into 2-inch chunks

3 garlic cloves, crushed

¾ cup cider vinegar

2 teaspoons salt

1 small onion, chopped fine

1 green bell pepper, chopped fine

2 tablespoons vegetable oil

2 vine-ripened tomatoes, chopped fine

2 tablespoons ketchup

1 tablespoon Dijon mustard

2 teaspoons sugar

½ teaspoon dried hot red pepper flakes

½ cup chopped fresh coriander sprigs

1 large bag tortilla chips (about 50)

In a heavy kettle barely cover pork with water and add garlic, ¼ cup vinegar, and 1 teaspoon salt. Simmer mixture, covered, 1 hour, or until pork is very tender.

While pork is simmering, in a large skillet cook onion and bell pepper in oil until onion is golden. Add tomatoes, ketchup, mustard, sugar, red pepper flakes, remaining ½ cup vinegar, and remaining teaspoon salt and simmer, stirring occasionally, 5 minutes.

Drain pork in a colander and return to kettle. Add sauce and mash pork with a potato masher or shred with 2 forks until shredded and combined well with sauce. Stir in coriander. *Pulled pork may be made 2 days ahead and cooled completely, uncovered, before being chilled, covered. Reheat pulled pork.*

Top each tortilla chip with 1 heaping teaspoon pulled pork.

Makes 3½ cups pulled pork, enough for 50 hors d'oeuvres with generous leftovers.

INDONESIAN PEANUT DIP WITH CRUDITÉS

===

¾ *cup sliced shallots*

2 garlic cloves, sliced

3 tablespoons vegetable oil

two 7-ounce jars roasted red peppers, drained and patted dry

⅓ *cup dry-roasted peanuts*

2 tablespoons tomato paste

1 tablespoon distilled vinegar

½ *teaspoon Tabasco*

ACCOMPANIMENTS:

5 Belgian endives, separated into leaves

1 bunch celery, cut into sticks

2 seedless cucumbers, seeded and cut into sticks

In a non-stick skillet cook shallots and garlic in oil over moderate heat, stirring, until golden. In a blender purée roasted peppers and peanuts until almost smooth. Add shallot mixture and remaining ingredients and blend until combined well. *Dip may be made 1 day ahead and chilled, covered.*

Serve dip with crudités.

Makes about 2 cups dip.

Photo on front jacket

STONE CRAB CLAWS WITH PARSLEY SAUCE

===

FOR SAUCE

1 cup packed fresh parsley leaves

¼ *cup bottled horseradish, drained*

3 tablespoons water

1 cup mayonnaise

1 tablespoon distilled vinegar

freshly ground white pepper to taste

24 large or 36 small cooked stone crab claws*, scrubbed if necessary

*available at some fish markets and by mail order (page 231)

Make sauce:

In a blender purée parsley and horseradish with water until smooth. In a bowl stir parsley mixture with remaining sauce ingredients and salt to taste until combined. *Sauce may be made 1 day ahead and chilled, covered.*

Crack crab claws with a mallet, leaving shells intact, and arrange on ice. Serve crab claws with sauce for dipping.

Serves 16 to 20 as an hors d'oeuvre.

Photo on front jacket

Menu

CHAMPAGNE PUNCH

LOBSTER-STUFFED TOMATOES

SPINACH-STUFFED MUSHROOMS

SALMON AND YOGURT TERRINE

━━━

BEEF TENDERLOINS
WITH JELLIED GAZPACHO

LAYERED COBB SALAD

ASPARAGUS WITH CURRY SAUCE

QUINOA AND FENNEL SALAD

*Château de Chamirey
Mercurey Blanc 1995*

Château Greysac Médoc 1993

━━━

FROZEN LEMON MERINGUE CAKES

Moët & Chandon Demi-Sec Champagne

SERVES 18 TO 24

Designed with an exquisite summer garden in mind, our anniversary party boasts lavish dishes that are ideal for serving out-of-doors. Pass the Lobster-Stuffed Tomatoes and Spinach-Stuffed Mushrooms and put out the Salmon and Yogurt Terrine (by the punch) for hors d'oeuvres; then, set out the other dishes on an elegant buffet for guests to serve themselves. For a pretty finale, we frosted our heavenly Frozen Lemon Meringue Cakes using a pastry bag fitted with a basketwork tip. If you prefer, simply swirl icing on the cakes with a spreader or knife.

SILVER ANNIVERSARY GARDEN PARTY

CHAMPAGNE PUNCH

═══

3 cups unsweetened pineapple juice

1½ cups triple sec

1½ cups brandy

¾ cup Chambord (black-raspberry liqueur)

1½ quarts ginger ale, chilled

three 750-ml. bottles dry Champagne, chilled

In a bowl stir together pineapple juice, triple sec, brandy, and Chambord. *Chill pineapple mixture, covered, at least 4 hours or overnight.* In a large punch bowl combine pineapple mixture, ginger ale, and Champagne and add ice cubes.

Makes about 24 cups.

Photo on page 176

LOBSTER-STUFFED TOMATOES

═══

½ pound cooked lobster meat or cooked shrimp, chopped fine

¼ cup mayonnaise

¼ cup finely chopped celery

¼ cup finely chopped fresh chives

2 teaspoons fresh lemon juice, or to taste

¼ teaspoon Tabasco, or to taste

2 pounds medium vine-ripened cherry tomatoes (about 70)

In a bowl stir together all ingredients except tomatoes until combined well and season with salt and pepper. *Chill filling, covered, while preparing tomatoes and up to 1 day.*

Cut ¼ inch from stem end of each tomato with a sharp knife and with a small melon-baller carefully scoop out pulp and seeds. Sprinkle tomato shells lightly with salt and invert onto paper towels. Drain shells 15 minutes.

Stuff tomato shells with filling, mounding it. *Tomatoes may be stuffed 6 hours ahead and chilled, covered.*

Makes about 70 hors d'oeuvres.

SPINACH-STUFFED MUSHROOMS

═══

two 10-ounce packages frozen chopped spinach

½ cup minced onion

1 large garlic clove, minced

4 tablespoons olive oil

½ pound baked ham, chopped fine

½ cup crumbled feta (about 3 ounces)

⅓ cup minced drained sun-dried tomatoes packed in oil

2 large eggs, beaten lightly

⅔ cup fine dry bread crumbs

1 teaspoon dried oregano, crumbled

4 pounds medium white mushrooms, stems discarded

Preheat oven to 400° F.

In a large saucepan cook frozen spinach in 1½ cups boiling water until just tender, about 3 minutes, and drain in a colander. Cool spinach and squeeze dry by handfuls.

In a skillet cook onion and garlic in 1 tablespoon oil over moderately low heat, stirring, until onion is softened. Remove skillet from heat and stir in spinach, ham, feta, tomatoes, eggs, bread crumbs, oregano, and salt and pepper to taste.

In a large bowl toss mushrooms with remaining 3 tablespoons oil to coat. Divide filling among mushrooms, mounding it, and arrange mushrooms in 2 large shallow baking pans. Bake mushrooms in upper and lower thirds of oven 15 minutes, or until heated through.

Makes about 70 hors d'oeuvres.

SALMON AND YOGURT TERRINE

=

7 cups plain yogurt (3½ pounds)

two ¼-ounce envelopes unflavored gelatin (about 5 teaspoons)

⅓ cup cold water

1 cup crème fraîche or heavy cream

2 teaspoons salt

½ pound smoked salmon, chopped coarse

⅓ cup drained small capers (about one 3-ounce jar), patted dry

⅓ cup chopped scallions including greens (about 3)

⅓ cup finely chopped fresh parsley leaves

¼ cup finely chopped fresh dill

⅔ cup salmon roe (about one 7-ounce jar)

GARNISH: *fresh parsley leaves, fresh dill sprigs, and lemon slices*

ACCOMPANIMENT: *melba toasts or crackers*

Put yogurt in a large sieve or colander lined with a double-thickness of well-rinsed and squeezed cheesecloth and set over a large bowl. *Drain yogurt, covered and chilled, at least 8 hours and up to 1 day.* Transfer yogurt to a large bowl.

Line each of 2 small loaf pans, 7½ by 3½ by 2 inches, with plastic wrap, leaving about a 2-inch overhang on long sides of pans.

In a saucepan sprinkle gelatin over ⅓ cup cold water and let stand until softened, about 5 minutes. Add *crème fraîche* or heavy cream and salt and heat over moderately low heat, stirring, just until gelatin is dissolved (do not boil). Whisk gelatin mixture into yogurt and stir in salmon, capers, scallions, parsley, dill, and black pepper to taste until combined well. Gently fold in salmon roe just until combined. Divide mixture between loaf pans and cover terrines with overhanging plastic wrap. *Chill terrines at least until firm enough to unmold, about 3 hours, and up to 2 days.*

Invert terrines onto platters, discarding plastic wrap, and garnish with parsley, dill, and lemon. Serve terrines with toasts or crackers.

Serves 18 to 24 as an hors d'oeuvre.

Beef Tenderloins with Jellied Gazpacho

===

2 trimmed 3½-pound beef tenderloins, tied
  and halved crosswise, at room
  temperature

about ⅓ cup cracked black pepper

3 tablespoons vegetable oil

three ¼-ounce envelopes unflavored gelatin
  (about 2½ tablespoons)

½ cup cold water

5 cups Pomì strained tomatoes (about one
  and a quarter 35-ounce cartons)

1½ cups finely chopped green bell pepper

1½ cups finely chopped peeled seeded
  cucumber

¾ cup finely chopped red onion

¼ cup chopped fresh parsley leaves

1 tablespoon sugar

2 teaspoons Worcestershire sauce

½ teaspoon finely grated fresh lemon zest

GARNISH: *watercress sprigs*

Preheat oven to 500° F.

Pat tenderloins dry and coat on all sides
with pepper. Season tenderloins with salt. In a
large flameproof roasting pan set over 2 burners
heat oil over moderately high heat until hot but
not smoking and brown tenderloins on all sides.
Roast tenderloins in middle of oven 15 to 17
minutes, or until a meat thermometer registers
130° F. for medium-rare. Transfer tenderloins
in pan to a rack and cool to room temperature.
*Tenderloins may be roasted 2 days ahead and
chilled, wrapped well. Bring tenderloins to room
temperature before slicing.*

Lightly oil a 9-cup non-reactive ring mold
(preferably plastic).

In a saucepan sprinkle gelatin over ½ cup
cold water and let stand until softened, about
5 minutes. Add 2 cups tomatoes and heat over
moderately low heat, stirring, until gelatin is
dissolved (do not boil). In a large bowl stir
together remaining 3 cups tomatoes, bell
pepper, cucumber, onion, parsley, sugar,
Worcestershire sauce, and zest. Stir in gelatin
mixture and salt and pepper to taste until
combined well and pour into mold. *Chill gazpacho mixture, covered with plastic wrap, at
least until firm enough to unmold, about 4
hours, and up to 2 days.*

Discard strings from tenderloin and cut
beef crosswise into ⅓-inch-thick slices.

Run a thin knife around inside of mold.
Dip mold in hot water 2 or 3 seconds and
invert a platter over mold. Invert mold with a
sharp rap to release jellied gazpacho. Cut jellied gazpacho into ⅓-inch-thick slices.

Arrange alternating slices of beef and jellied gazpacho on a large platter and garnish
with watercress.

Serves 18 to 24.

Layered Cobb Salad

===

FOR DRESSING
  ½ cup fresh grapefruit juice
  ½ cup red-wine vinegar
  3 tablespoons Dijon mustard
  2 cups olive oil

FOR SALAD

1 head romaine, chopped (about 8 cups)

1 head Boston lettuce, chopped
(about 8 cups)

1 pound fresh spinach, coarse stems
discarded and leaves chopped
(about 5 cups)

1 bunch watercress, coarse stems discarded
and sprigs chopped (about 3 cups)

5 ripe California avocados

2 tablespoons fresh lemon juice

½ pound cooked bacon, crumbled

a 3-pound piece smoked boneless turkey or
chicken breast, cut into ¼-inch dice

½ cup thinly sliced scallion

3 vine-ripened tomatoes, seeded and chopped

1¼ cups crumbled Roquefort
(about 8 ounces)

1 hard-boiled large egg

Make dressing:

In a bowl whisk together grapefruit juice,
vinegar, mustard, and salt and pepper to taste
and add oil in a slow stream, whisking until
emulsified. *Dressing may be made 1 day ahead
and chilled, covered.*

Make salad:

*Note: All salad ingredients except avocados
and egg may be prepared 1 day ahead and
chilled separately in sealable bags.*

In a large bowl toss together romaine,
Boston lettuce, spinach, and watercress.

Halve and pit avocados. Peel avocados
and cut into ½-inch pieces. In a bowl toss
avocados with lemon juice.

Divide mixed greens between two 20-inch
oval platters to cover completely. On top of
greens arrange layers of bacon, avocados,

turkey or chicken, scallion, tomatoes, and
Roquefort. Force egg through a fine sieve into
a small bowl and sprinkle on top of Roquefort.

Whisk dressing well and serve salad with
dressing on the side.

Serves 18 to 24.

ASPARAGUS WITH CURRY SAUCE

8 pounds medium asparagus, trimmed

2 cups mayonnaise

1 tablespoon curry powder

1 teaspoon minced peeled fresh gingerroot

2 tablespoons fresh lemon juice

¼ to ½ cup milk

In a large kettle of boiling salted water cook
asparagus in batches until tender but not
limp, about 5 minutes, transferring carefully
with tongs to a colander to drain. Transfer
asparagus to a platter and cool.

In a bowl whisk together remaining ingredients, using enough milk to reach desired
consistency, until combined well.

Serve asparagus with sauce on the side.

Serves 18 to 24.

QUINOA AND FENNEL SALAD

===

4 cups quinoa*

4 cups seedless red grapes, halved

3 cups finely chopped fennel bulbs

1½ cups slivered almonds, toasted lightly

⅓ cup chopped fresh parsley leaves

3 tablespoons chopped fresh thyme leaves

3 tablespoons chopped fresh tarragon leaves

½ cup red-wine vinegar

½ cup olive oil

2 teaspoons salt

*available at natural foods stores

In a bowl wash quinoa in at least 5 changes cold water, rubbing grains and letting them settle before pouring off most water, until water runs clear and drain in a large fine sieve or a large metal colander lined with cheesecloth.

In a kettle of boiling salted water cook quinoa 10 minutes. Drain quinoa in sieve or colander lined with cheesecloth and rinse under cold water. In kettle bring ½ inch water to a boil and set sieve or colander in kettle (quinoa should not touch water). Steam quinoa, covered with a towel and lid, until fluffy and dry, about 10 minutes (check water level occasionally, adding water if necessary).

Transfer quinoa to a bowl and cool. Add remaining ingredients and pepper to taste. *Salad may be made 1 day ahead and chilled, covered. Bring salad to room temperature.*

Serves 18 to 24.

FROZEN LEMON MERINGUE CAKES

===

FOR MERINGUE LAYERS

8 large egg whites at room temperature

2 cups sugar

6 cups lemon cream (recipe follows)

FOR ICING

1 tablespoon unflavored gelatin

⅓ cup orange-flavored liqueur such as Grand Marnier

3 cups well-chilled heavy cream

GARNISH: *lemon slices and unsprayed lemon leaves*

ACCOMPANIMENT: *fresh raspberries*

Make meringue layers:

Preheat oven to 275° F. Butter 2 large baking sheets and line with parchment or foil. On each sheet trace 2 squares, using bottom of a 9-inch square cake pan as a guide.

In a large bowl with an electric mixer beat whites with a pinch salt until they hold soft peaks and add sugar, 1 tablespoon at a time, beating until whites hold stiff, glossy peaks. Transfer meringue to a pastry bag fitted with a ½-inch plain tip. Pipe meringue to fill in squares and smooth tops.

Bake meringue layers in upper and lower thirds of oven 1 hour, switching position of pans halfway through baking, or until firm when touched lightly and very pale golden. Remove meringues on parchment from baking sheets and cool on racks. Peel off parchment carefully. With a serrated knife trim 2 meringue layers to fit inside bottoms of two 9-inch square cake pans and trim remaining 2 layers to fit inside tops of pans. Crumble trimmings and reserve.

Oil pans with vegetable oil and line with plastic wrap, leaving about a 5-inch overhang on all sides. Put smaller meringue layers, smooth sides down, in lined pans. Stir reserved meringue crumbs into lemon cream and divide between pans, smoothing it. Top filling with remaining meringue layers, smooth sides up, pressing gently. Fold plastic wrap over tops to enclose cakes. *Freeze cakes, wrapped well, at least until frozen solid, about 8 hours and up to 3 days.*

Make icing:

In a small saucepan sprinkle gelatin over liqueur and let stand until softened, about 5 minutes. Heat mixture over low heat, stirring, until gelatin is dissolved (do not boil). In a bowl beat cream until it just holds soft peaks and add gelatin mixture in a stream, beating until icing holds stiff peaks.

Unwrap cakes and unmold each onto a serving plate, discarding plastic wrap. Spread a thin even layer of icing on tops and sides of cakes. Transfer remaining icing to a pastry bag fitted with a decorative tip (such as a basketwork tip) and pipe over cakes. *Cakes may be iced 1½ hours ahead and chilled, uncovered.*

Garnish cakes with lemon slices and leaves. Serve cakes, cut into squares with a serrated knife, with raspberries.

Photo above

Lemon Cream

2 sticks (1 cup) unsalted butter
1½ cups sugar
1 teaspoon cornstarch
1 cup fresh lemon juice (from about 4 lemons)
2 tablespoons freshly grated lemon zest
2 whole large eggs
12 large egg yolks
2 cups plain yogurt

In a heavy saucepan heat butter, sugar, cornstarch, lemon juice, and zest over moderately low heat, stirring, until sugar is dissolved. In a bowl lightly whisk together whole eggs and yolks and add hot butter mixture in a stream, whisking. Transfer mixture to pan and cook over moderately low heat, whisking constantly, 3 to 5 minutes, or until curd holds mark of whisk and first bubbles appear on surface. Transfer curd immediately to a bowl and cover surface with plastic wrap. Cool curd. *Chill curd, covered, at least until cold, about 1 hour, and up to 2 days.* Whisk yogurt into curd.

Makes about 6 cups.

4

GETAWAY PARTIES

Crisp fall days are made for apple-picking or leaf-peeping, and toting along a picnic makes outings even more special. Our menu is both ample and sophisticated, with a warming pumpkin soup, sourdough rolls, a smoked turkey entrée salad, and a rustic, free-form galette. Undetectable shortcuts, such as canned pumpkin for the soup and deli turkey breast for the salad, help out the cook. We've kept portability in mind too: The soup stays warm in a thermos; the salad travels in separate plastic containers or bags (one each for the arugula, couscous, turkey salad, and nuts); and the galette, made with a sturdy dough, transports well if kept flat in a pie-carrier or flat-bottomed basket with handles. You may also want to bring along another thermos of piping-hot coffee to serve with dessert.

♦ Soup may be made 2 days ahead.

♦ Galette may be made 6 hours ahead.

AN APPLE
ORCHARD PICNIC

Pumpkin Soup with Shallots and Sage

½ cup minced shallots

2 tablespoons unsalted butter

½ teaspoon turmeric

½ teaspoon dried sage, crumbled

1 bay leaf

1 tablespoon cider vinegar

a 15-ounce can solid-pack pumpkin

5 cups chicken broth

½ cup heavy cream

¼ cup minced fresh chives

In a heavy kettle cook shallots in butter over moderate heat, stirring occasionally, until golden brown. Add turmeric, sage, bay leaf, and vinegar and cook, stirring, 1 minute. Add pumpkin and broth and simmer, stirring occasionally, 15 minutes. Discard bay leaf and in a blender purée mixture in batches until very smooth (use caution when blending hot liquids), transferring to a large saucepan. Stir in cream and salt and pepper to taste. *Soup may be made 2 days ahead and cooled completely, uncovered, before being chilled, covered.* Cook soup over moderate heat until hot and stir in chives. Keep soup warm in a large thermos.

Makes about 7 cups, serving 4 generously.

Smoked Turkey Salad with Grapes, Couscous, and Arugula

1⅔ cups water

1 cup couscous

½ teaspoon ground cumin

1½ tablespoons minced fresh parsley leaves

a ¾-pound piece smoked boneless turkey breast, cut into ¾-inch cubes

2½ cups seedless red grapes (about 1 pound), halved

¼ cup fresh red or pink grapefruit juice

1 tablespoon fresh lemon juice

½ cup packed fresh basil leaves, cut into thin strips

1 bunch arugula (about 2 cups packed), coarse stems discarded

¼ cup walnuts, toasted and chopped

In a saucepan bring water to a boil and stir in couscous. Let couscous stand, covered, 5 minutes. Stir in cumin, parsley, and salt to taste with a fork and cool to room temperature.

In a bowl toss together turkey, grapes, citrus juices, basil, and salt and pepper to taste. Arrange arugula on 4 plates and top with couscous and turkey salad, drizzling any liquid remaining in bowl over salads. Sprinkle salads with walnuts.

Serves 4.

Apple Galette

═══

FOR PASTRY DOUGH

¼ *cup confectioners' sugar*

1½ *cups all-purpose flour*

1 *teaspoon salt*

1½ *sticks cold unsalted butter, cut into bits*

1 *large egg yolk*

2 *tablespoons cold water*

4 *medium Gala or Empire apples*

¼ *cup white wine*

⅓ *cup granulated sugar*

FOR GLAZE

½ *cup white wine*

½ *cup apple jelly*

¼ *cup loosely packed fresh thyme sprigs*

GARNISH: *fresh thyme sprigs and leaves*

Make dough:

In a bowl stir together confectioners' sugar, flour, and salt. With a pastry blender or your fingertips blend in butter until mixture resembles coarse meal. In a small bowl stir together yolk and cold water. Add yolk mixture, 1 tablespoon at a time, to flour mixture, tossing until mixture forms a dough. On a work surface smear dough in 3 or 4 forward motions with heel of hand to make dough easier to work with. Form dough into a ball and flatten to form a 1-inch-thick disk. *Chill dough, wrapped in plastic wrap, at least 30 minutes and up to 1 day.*

Halve and core apples (do not peel) and cut crosswise into ¼-inch-thick slices. In a large bowl toss apples gently with wine.

Preheat oven to 400° F.

On a lightly floured surface roll out dough into a 15-inch round and transfer to a large baking sheet. Fold in edge 1 inch all around to form a border. Arrange slices on pastry round in overlapping concentric circles. Brush slices and pastry border with wine remaining in bowl and sprinkle with granulated sugar.

Bake *galette* 45 minutes, or until apples are tender and pastry is golden, and cool on baking sheet on a rack.

Make glaze while *galette* is cooling:

In a small saucepan simmer wine and jelly with thyme until liquid is reduced by half, about 15 minutes.

Discard thyme with a slotted spoon and brush hot glaze generously over apples. Garnish *galette* with thyme sprigs and leaves. *Galette may be made 6 hours ahead and kept, loosely covered, at room temperature.*

Photo on page 186

Since seafood is bound to be fresh and delicious at the shore, why not serve it as often as possible while you are there? Our luncheon calls for mussels and swordfish, so be sure to shop early in the day for both. Look for tightly closed mussels that are free of barnacles or seaweed, which may indicate they are sandy. For more flavorful swordfish, choose a steak with a pinkish hue; avoid those with dark spots, which are oily-tasting. The berry puddings, made by combining a simple fresh berry compote with cubes of store-bought pound cake, are one of the most delightful shortcut desserts in this book.

◆ Dressing may be made 1 day ahead.

◆ Puddings must be chilled at least 2 hours and up to 1 day.

◆ Lemonade keeps, chilled, 6 hours.

A BEACH HOUSE LUNCH

MINTED PEACH LEMONADE

1 cup loosely packed fresh mint leaves
⅔ cup sugar
1 cup fresh lemon juice (from about 4 lemons)
3 cups water
1 cup canned peach nectar, chilled

GARNISH: *peach slices and fresh mint sprigs*

In a bowl bruise mint leaves in sugar with back of a spoon. Stir in lemon juice and water, stirring until sugar is dissolved. Pour mixture through a sieve into a pitcher and stir in peach nectar. *Lemonade may be made 6 hours ahead and chilled, covered.*

Serve lemonade over ice in tall glasses, garnished with peach slices and mint sprigs.

Makes about 6 cups.

Steamed Mussels with Orange, Fennel, and Garlic

1 navel orange

2 large garlic cloves, minced and mashed to a paste with ½ teaspoon salt

2 shallots, chopped fine (about ⅓ cup)

½ cup finely chopped fennel bulb (sometimes called anise)

1 teaspoon fennel seeds

2 tablespoons unsalted butter

¼ cup dry white wine

½ cup chicken broth

1 pound mussels (preferably cultivated), scrubbed well and beards pulled off

1 tablespoon chopped fresh parsley leaves

With a vegetable peeler remove three 3- by ½-inch strips orange zest. Cut remaining peel and pith from orange with a sharp knife and discard. Cut out fruit sections from between membranes, discarding membranes, and finely chop enough fruit to measure ⅓ cup, reserving remaining fruit for another use.

In a large saucepan with a tight-fitting lid cook garlic paste, shallots, chopped fennel, and fennel seeds in butter over moderate heat, uncovered, stirring, until chopped fennel is softened, about 5 minutes. Stir in wine and zest and boil 1 minute. Add broth and return to a boil. Add mussels and cook, covered, over high heat, checking them every minute, 3 to 8 minutes, and transferring them as they open with a slotted spoon to a serving

bowl. (Discard any mussels that are unopened after 8 minutes.)

Into broth stir chopped orange, parsley, and salt and pepper to taste and spoon over mussels.

Serves 4 as an hors d'oeuvre.

Photo on page 190

Tips for Grilling

To start a charcoal fire we prefer to use a chimney starter, also called a metal flue. This is a safe, inexpensive tool that won't impart a petroleum taste to foods.

To use the chimney starter: Stuff 2 crumpled sheets of newspaper into bottom section, beneath grid, and set chimney on grill's bottom or grate. Fill top section with charcoal, about three-fourths full. Light newspaper through holes around bottom of chimney to ignite coals and allow them to burn until grayish-white in color, about 25 minutes. Carefully empty out coals, spreading them in a single layer. Arrange coals close together in center of grill for a hot area; leave some space between coals along edge for a cool area.

Prevent foods from sticking to the grill by preheating the grill rack for at least 5 minutes. Using a long-handled basting brush lightly oil the rack, and brush foods with oil. Turn foods only once, with tongs, about halfway through cooking.

SWORDFISH SOUVLAKI

===

1 pound skinless swordfish steak (about 1 inch thick), cut into 1-inch cubes

1 tablespoon fresh lemon juice

½ teaspoon dried oregano, crumbled

four 6- to 7-inch pita loaves (preferably pocketless)

1 large cucumber

an 8-ounce container plain yogurt

1½ teaspoons chopped fresh mint leaves

½ teaspoon chopped garlic, mashed to a paste with ½ teaspoon salt

2 medium plum tomatoes, chopped coarse

½ small red onion, cut into slivers

¼ cup fresh flat-leafed parsley leaves, torn into pieces

four 12-inch bamboo skewers, soaked in water 1 hour

Prepare grill. Preheat oven to 200° F.

In a bowl toss swordfish with lemon juice, oregano, and salt and pepper to taste and marinate, covered and chilled, 15 minutes.

Wrap pitas in foil and warm in oven. Peel and seed cucumber and coarsely grate. Wrap cucumber in a kitchen towel and squeeze out liquid. In a small bowl stir together cucumber, yogurt, mint, garlic paste, and salt and pepper to taste. In another bowl combine tomatoes, onion, parsley, and salt and pepper to taste.

Thread fish onto skewers and grill on an oiled rack set 5 to 6 inches over glowing coals, turning once, until just cooked through, about 8 minutes. (Alternatively, grill fish in a hot well-seasoned ridged grill pan.) Remove fish from skewers.

Divide cucumber mixture among pitas, spreading to cover, and top with fish. Sprinkle tomato mixture over fish and roll pitas into cones, wrapping with parchment paper or foil to secure.

Serves 4.

Photo above

TOSSED SALAD WITH ROSEMARY FETA DRESSING

FOR DRESSING

⅓ cup crumbled feta (about 2 ounces)

2 tablespoons water

1 tablespoon fresh lemon juice

1 tablespoon mayonnaise

1 tablespoon honey

1½ teaspoons chopped fresh rosemary leaves
   or ½ teaspoon dried rosemary, crumbled

½ teaspoon coarsely ground black pepper

2 tablespoons vegetable oil

1 large head romaine, torn into bite-size
   pieces (about 8 cups)

½ medium red onion, sliced thin

⅓ cup sliced Kalamata olives

Make dressing:

In a blender blend together all ingredients except oil until smooth and with motor running add oil in a stream, blending until emulsified. *Dressing may be made 1 day ahead and chilled, covered. Bring dressing to room temperature before using.*

In a large bowl toss together romaine, onion, olives, and dressing.

Serves 4.

BERRY AND POUND CAKE PUDDINGS

1 pint raspberries and/or blackberries,
   picked over

1 cup red wine

¼ cup sugar

2 tablespoons cornstarch

six ½-inch-thick slices plain pound cake, cut
   into ½-inch cubes

4 scoops vanilla frozen yogurt (about 1 pint)

In a small saucepan simmer berries in wine 1 minute, or until berries are tender but still hold their shape. Drain berries in a sieve set over a bowl, reserving berry liquid, and transfer berries to a large bowl. In a small bowl whisk together sugar and cornstarch and gradually add reserved liquid, whisking until smooth. Transfer mixture to saucepan and simmer, stirring, 5 minutes, or until thickened. Add sauce and cake cubes to berries and toss gently to combine. Divide pudding among 4 bowls. *Chill puddings, covered, at least until cold, about 2 hours, and up to 1 day.*

Serve puddings topped with frozen yogurt.

Serves 4.

After many years, fondue is back as a chic, fun party food. (So dust off your fondue pots, or look for one at a garage sale.) We think it's an ideal choice for an intimate party, especially after a bone-chilling day on the slopes. Our "new" version includes chipotle chilies for a smoky-flavored, spicy kick. And, in addition to the expected bread cubes, we suggest bread sticks and cooked vegetables—broccoli flowerets, carrot sticks, pearl onions, even tiny new potatoes—for dipping. The salad can be made in a snap if you make the spiced nuts ahead and wash and store the greens. (To make extra nuts for nibbling, just double the recipe.)

◆ Nuts for the salad may be made 1 week ahead.

◆ Brownie cake may be made 1 day ahead.

APRÈS-SKI SPICY FONDUE

CHIPOTLE CHEESE FONDUE

===

½ pound finely diced Gruyère cheese (about 2 cups)

½ pound finely diced Emmenthal cheese (about 2 cups)

1½ tablespoons cornstarch

2 large garlic cloves, halved

1⅓ cups dry white wine

1 tablespoon fresh lemon juice

2 tablespoons kirsch, or to taste

freshly grated nutmeg to taste if desired

3 canned chipotle chilies in adobo*, or to taste, minced (about 1½ tablespoons)

fried shallots (recipe follows)

⅔ cup thinly sliced scallion greens if desired

4 slices cooked bacon, crumbled, if desired

ACCOMPANIMENTS:

cooked vegetables such as broccoli flowerets, carrot sticks, pearl onions, and potatoes

breadsticks (store-bought)

cubes of day-old French or Italian bread

*available at Latino markets and by mail order (page 231)

In a bowl toss together cheeses and cornstarch.

Rub inside of a 3- to 4-quart heavy saucepan with garlic halves, leaving garlic in pan, and add wine and lemon juice. Bring liquid just to a boil and add cheese mixture by handfuls, stirring. Bring mixture to a bare simmer over moderate heat, stirring, and stir in kirsch, nutmeg, chilies, and pepper to taste.

Transfer fondue to a fondue pot and keep warm over a low flame. Stir in fried shallots and scallion greens and/or bacon and serve fondue with accompaniments for dipping. (Stir fondue often to keep combined.)

Serves 4.

Photo on page 196

FRIED SHALLOTS

1½ cups thinly sliced shallots (about 8 large)

4 tablespoons vegetable oil

In a 10- to 12-inch heavy skillet cook shallots in oil over moderately high heat, stirring, until golden brown. Transfer shallots with a slotted spoon to paper towels to drain and season with salt.

Makes about ⅔ cup.

MIXED GREENS SALAD

FOR NUTS

1 cup walnuts

½ teaspoon sugar

½ teaspoon coarse salt

¼ teaspoon ground cumin

¼ teaspoon ground coriander seeds

1½ teaspoons unsalted butter, melted

2 tablespoons bottled red grape juice

1 tablespoon red-wine vinegar

2 tablespoons vegetable oil

½ *tart green apple*

1 medium head chicory, torn into pieces

1 large Belgian endive, sliced crosswise

½ *bunch watercress, coarse stems discarded*

Make spiced walnuts:

Preheat oven to 350° F.

Spread nuts on a baking sheet and toast in middle of oven until golden, about 8 minutes. While nuts are toasting, in a bowl toss together remaining nut ingredients. Add nuts and toss to coat. *Nuts may be made 1 week ahead and chilled in an airtight container. Reheat nuts in a preheated 350° F. oven.*

In a large bowl whisk together juice, vinegar, oil, and salt and pepper to taste. Peel apple and cut into ½-inch pieces. Add apple and greens to vinaigrette and toss until coated.

Serve salad sprinkled with warm nuts.

Serves 4.

BROWNIE CAKE

4 *large eggs*

½ *cup granulated sugar*

4 *tablespoons water*

½ *teaspoon salt*

¾ *teaspoon vanilla*

1 *cup chocolate wafer crumbs (18 wafers)*

½ *cup semisweet chocolate chips*

½ *stick unsalted butter, melted and cooled*

½ *cup packed dark brown sugar*

1 *cup graham cracker crumbs (8 crackers)*

⅓ *cup chopped pecans*

Preheat oven to 350° F. and butter an 8-inch square baking pan.

In a bowl whisk together 2 eggs, granulated sugar, 2 tablespoons water, ¼ teaspoon salt, and ¼ teaspoon vanilla until smooth and stir in chocolate wafer crumbs, chocolate chips, and half of butter. In another bowl whisk together remaining 2 eggs, brown sugar, remaining 2 tablespoons water, remaining ¼ teaspoon salt, and remaining ½ teaspoon vanilla until smooth and stir in graham cracker crumbs, pecans, and remaining 2 tablespoons butter. (Batters will be thin.) Working quickly, drop large spoonfuls of each batter alternately into baking pan and run a knife through batters to marbleize.

Bake cake in middle of oven 35 minutes, or until a tester comes out clean and cool in pan on a rack 10 minutes. Cut cake into 16 squares and cool completely. *Cake may be made 1 day ahead and kept covered at room temperature.*

Makes 16 squares.

Photo below

GRAPEFRUIT RUM COOLERS

CURRIED COCONUT CHIPS

■

PENNE, SPINACH, AND HAM PIE

SLICED TOMATOES AND MOZZARELLA
WITH THREE-HERB PESTO

MARINATED CAULIFLOWER
AND CARROT SALAD

■

PEANUT ICEBOX COOKIES

FRESH FRUIT

Nipozzano Chianti Riserva 1993

SERVES 8

S ailing is one of the quickest ways to unwind, and our lunch afloat is just as relaxing. Welcome your guests aboard with refreshing grapefruit rum coolers and curried coconut chips. For lunch, the salads are simple and delicious and we promise rave reviews for our impressive pasta pie (although it is time consuming to prepare). Ideally, make the pie dough in advance, then assemble and bake the pie the day before you set out.

◆ Cookie dough must be frozen at least 1 hour and up to 2 weeks.

◆ Pesto for tomato salad may be made 1 week ahead.

◆ Chips may be made 4 days ahead.

◆ Pasta pie dough must be chilled at least 1 hour and up to 1 day. Pie may be made 1 day ahead.

◆ Vegetable salad must marinate at least 1 hour and up to 1 day.

◆ Grapefruit mixture for coolers may be made up to 4 hours ahead.

LUNCH AFLOAT

COOLERS

16 fresh mint leaves
¼ cup superfine sugar, or to taste
6 tablespoons fresh lemon or lime juice
1½ cups light rum, or to taste
2⅔ cups fresh grapefruit juice
fresh club soda or seltzer, chilled
Angostura bitters

GARNISH: *grapefruit wedges and mint sprigs*

In a large bowl with back of a spoon bruise mint with sugar and lemon or lime juice until sugar is dissolved. Add rum and grapefruit juice and strain into a large thermos or plastic pitcher with sealable lid. *Coolers may be prepared up to this point 4 hours ahead and chilled, covered.*

Fill 8 ice-filled tall glasses three-fourths full with grapefruit mixture and top off drinks with club soda and a splash of bitters. Stir drinks and garnish with grapefruit and mint.

Makes 8 drinks.

Photo above

CURRIED COCONUT CHIPS

═

1 coconut (no cracks and containing liquid)
2 teaspoons curry powder
1½ teaspoons salt
1 teaspoon sugar
¼ teaspoon cayenne
¼ teaspoon freshly ground black pepper

Preheat oven to 400° F.

Pierce the softest eye of coconut with an ice pick or skewer and drain liquid. Bake coconut in oven 15 minutes and on a work surface break open with a hammer. With point of a small knife carefully pry flesh out of shell and cut into large pieces. With a vegetable peeler shave coconut along cut edges into thin strips.

Reduce temperature to 350° F.

In a bowl stir together remaining ingredients and add coconut strips. Toss mixture well and spread in one layer in 2 large shallow baking pans. Bake chips in upper and lower thirds of oven, switching position of pans halfway through baking and stirring occasionally, 15 to 20 minutes, or until crisp and beginning to turn golden. *Chips keep in an airtight container at room temperature 4 days.*

Makes about 3 cups.

Photo above

SLICED TOMATOES AND MOZZARELLA

4 large vine-ripened tomatoes, sliced
1 pound fresh mozzarella, sliced thin
½ cup three-herb pesto (recipe follows)
freshly ground black pepper to taste

GARNISH: *basil, mint, and/or parsley sprigs*

On a large round platter alternate tomato and mozzarella slices, overlapping slightly, and spoon pesto in a ring around center. Season tomatoes and mozzarella with pepper and garnish with herbs.

Serves 8.

Photo on page 200

THREE-HERB PESTO

⅔ cup packed fresh basil leaves
⅔ cup packed fresh mint leaves
⅔ cup packed fresh parsley leaves
⅓ cup pine nuts
⅓ cup freshly grated Parmesan
2 large garlic cloves, minced and mashed to a paste with ½ teaspoon salt
½ cup olive oil
1 tablespoon balsamic vinegar, or to taste

In a blender or food processor purée all ingredients with salt and pepper to taste until smooth. *Pesto keeps, chilled in a jar, 1 week.*

Makes about 1 cup.

MARINATED CAULIFLOWER AND CARROT SALAD

4 carrots, cut diagonally into ¼-inch-thick slices
1 head cauliflower, cut into 1-inch flowerets
2 celery ribs, cut diagonally into ½-inch-thick slices
½ cup extra-virgin olive oil
2 tablespoons red-wine vinegar
2 large garlic cloves, minced
½ teaspoon dried hot red pepper flakes, or to taste
a 2-inch strip lemon zest removed with a vegetable peeler and cut crosswise into thin julienne strips

In a kettle of boiling salted water cook carrots and cauliflower 2 minutes. Add celery and boil 2 minutes more. In a colander drain vegetables and rinse briefly under cold water. Drain vegetables well and transfer to a large bowl.

In a small bowl whisk together oil, vinegar, garlic, red pepper flakes, zest, and salt and pepper to taste until combined well and pour over vegetables. *Marinate vegetables, covered and chilled, at least 1 hour and up to 1 day.*

Serves 8.

PENNE, SPINACH, AND HAM PIE

━━

FOR DOUGH

>   2½ cups all-purpose flour
>   1½ sticks (¾ cup) cold unsalted butter, cut
>   into 12 pieces
>   1 teaspoon salt
>   6 to 8 tablespoons ice water

FOR FILLING

>   two 10-ounce packages frozen chopped
>   spinach, thawed
>   1 onion, chopped
>   1 garlic clove, minced
>   2 tablespoons unsalted butter
>   3 tablespoons all-purpose flour
>   2 cups milk
>   freshly grated nutmeg to taste
>   2 large eggs, beaten lightly
>   1 pound baked ham, cut into ½-inch cubes
>   1 cup pimiento-stuffed small green olives
>   (about a 5¾-ounce jar)
>   1 cup whole-milk ricotta
>   ½ cup freshly grated Parmesan
>   ¼ cup chopped fresh basil leaves
>   1 teaspoon minced fresh thyme leaves or
>   ½ teaspoon dried thyme, crumbled
>   10 ounces penne
>
>   1 large egg, beaten lightly

Make dough:

In a food processor pulse together flour, butter, and salt until mixture resembles coarse meal. Add 6 tablespoons ice water and pulse until incorporated. Add additional ice water if necessary, 1 tablespoon at a time, pulsing to incorporate, until mixture begins to form a dough. Divide dough into 2 pieces, one twice the size of the other, and form each piece into a ball. *Chill dough, each piece wrapped separately in wax paper, at least 1 hour and up to 1 day.*

Make filling:

Drain thawed spinach in a colander and squeeze dry by handfuls.

In a heavy saucepan cook onion and garlic in butter over moderate heat, stirring occasionally, until onion is pale golden. Add flour and cook *roux* over moderately low heat, stirring, about 3 minutes. Add milk in a stream, whisking, and bring to a boil. Simmer sauce, whisking, 2 minutes and transfer to a large heatproof bowl. Season sauce with nutmeg and stir in 2 eggs, ham, olives, ricotta, Parmesan, herbs, spinach, and salt and pepper to taste until combined well.

In a kettle of boiling salted water cook *penne* until *al dente*, about 8 minutes, and drain in a colander. Rinse *penne* briefly under cold water and drain well. Stir *penne* into sauce.

Preheat oven to 425° F.

On a lightly floured surface roll out larger piece of dough into an 18-inch round and fit into a 10-inch springform pan, trimming overhang to 1 inch. Brush bottom and sides of pie shell with some of beaten egg and pour filling into shell, tamping it down.

On lightly floured surface roll out remaining piece of dough into an 11-inch round. Drape dough over filling and crimp edges together decoratively. Brush top with beaten egg and prick decoratively all over with a fork.

Bake pie in middle of oven 10 minutes. Reduce temperature to 375° F. and bake pie 40 minutes more, or until top is golden. Cool pie in pan on a rack 10 minutes before serving. *Pie may be made 1 day ahead and cooled completely before being chilled, in pan, covered. Bring pie to room temperature before serving.* Serve pie hot or at room temperature.

Serves 8.

HANDLING HERBS

TO STORE FRESH HERBS

All herbs should be stored, unwashed, in airtight plastic bags in the refrigerator. Coriander, usually sold with roots intact, should be refrigerated in water with only roots submerged and leaves loosely covered with a plastic bag. Basil is fragile, so purchase or pick only as needed.

TO DRY AND STORE HERBS

If you have an herb garden you may want to dry your own herbs. To avoid moisture, pick herbs on a dry day. Tie herbs in bunches and hang them upside down in a dry, dimly lit, well-ventilated place at warm room temperature. When herbs are dry (about 1 week), strip leaves whole from their stems and store, covered, in jars. After 1 day, check leaves for condensation; if necessary, air-dry leaves on a baking sheet 12 hours more.

PEANUT ICEBOX COOKIES

1 stick (½ cup) unsalted butter, softened
½ cup packed light brown sugar
1 large egg
1 teaspoon vanilla
1½ cups all-purpose flour
½ teaspoon baking soda
¼ teaspoon salt
¾ cup finely chopped salted cocktail peanuts (not dry-roasted; about 4 ounces)
2 tablespoons granulated sugar

In a bowl with an electric mixer beat together butter and brown sugar until light and fluffy. Beat in egg and vanilla until smooth and beat in flour, baking soda, salt, and peanuts until combined well. On a sheet of wax paper form dough into a log about 1½ inches in diameter, using paper as a guide. *Freeze log, wrapped in wax paper, at least until firm, about 1 hour, and up to 2 weeks. Let log soften slightly before cutting.*

Preheat oven to 350° F.

Cut log into ⅛-inch-thick rounds and arrange about ¾ inch apart on 2 baking sheets. Sprinkle cookies with sugar.

Bake cookies in upper and lower thirds of oven, switching position of sheets halfway through baking, 10 minutes, or until golden around edges. Transfer cookies to racks to cool.

Makes about 40 cookies.

Tailgate parties mustn't be confused with picnics—the former are far more elegant, and, in some circles, require the use of genuine crystal, china, and flatware. After all, your car does all the toting so anything is possible, even candlesticks and wine coolers! Our portable feast offers updated traditional favorites, such as Bloody Marys, potted shrimp, and a goat cheese tart, that promise to satisfy your spectator friends. Ideally, transport both the drinks and soup in thermoses.

◆ Goat cheese tart: Pastry dough must be chilled at least 1 hour and up to 3 days; tart may be made 4 hours ahead.

◆ Shrimp must be chilled at least 1 hour and up to 2 days.

◆ Bars may be made 2 days ahead.

◆ Drinks may be made 1 day ahead.

◆ Soup may be made 1 day ahead.

◆ Vegetables for salad may be steamed 1 day ahead.

SPICY BLOODY MARYS

POTTED SHRIMP SCAMPI

▬

HEARTY VEGETABLE SOUP

GOAT CHEESE, POLENTA, AND MUSHROOM TART

POTATO AND GREEN BEAN SALAD WITH CITRUS MISO DRESSING

▬

CHEWY HAZELNUT BARS

▬

Ravenswood Vintners' Blend
California Zinfandel 1994

SERVES 6

TAILGATE PARTY AT THE GAME

POTTED SHRIMP SCAMPI

¾ *pound shrimp with shells*
2 *garlic cloves, halved*
1 *bay leaf, crumbled*
¼ *teaspoon celery seed*
1 *stick (½ cup) unsalted butter*
½ *teaspoon fresh lemon juice*
⅛ *teaspoon cayenne*
2 *tablespoons minced fresh parsley leaves*

ACCOMPANIMENT: *crackers or toast points*

Shell and devein shrimp, reserving shells. In a heavy skillet cook reserved shells, garlic, bay leaf, and celery seed in butter over moderately low heat, stirring, 6 minutes, or until shells are pink and garlic begins to turn golden. In a food processor pulse shell mixture until finely ground and pour through a fine sieve into skillet, pressing hard on solids. Discard solids. Add shrimp to shrimp butter and cook over moderate heat, stirring, until shrimp are cooked through, about 3 minutes. Transfer shrimp with a slotted spoon to cleaned food processor and pulse until coarsely ground. Add shrimp butter from skillet, lemon juice, cayenne, and salt to taste and pulse until shrimp is finely ground but not completely smooth. Transfer shrimp to a bowl and stir in parsley. *Chill potted shrimp, covered, at least until firm, about 1 hour, and up to 2 days.*

Serve potted shrimp with crackers or toasts.

Makes about 1¼ cups.

SPICY BLOODY MARYS

a 32-ounce bottle V-8 Spicy Hot vegetable juice, chilled
1 *cup lemon-flavored vodka or vodka*
3 *tablespoons fresh lemon juice*
1 *tablespoon fresh orange juice*
1 *tablespoon Worcestershire sauce*
½ *teaspoon celery salt*

In a large thermos combine all ingredients. *Bloody Marys may be made 1 day ahead and chilled, covered.* Just before serving, add 1 cup ice cubes to Bloody Marys and shake. Serve Bloody Marys over ice.

Makes 6 drinks.

VEGETABLE SOUP

4 *medium leeks (white and pale green parts only), chopped, washed well, and drained*
¼ *cup olive oil*
¾ *pound Jerusalem artichokes (also called sunchokes) or boiling potatoes*
6 *cups beef broth*
½ *cup dry red wine*
3 *cups chopped bok choy or escarole*
2 *medium zucchini, chopped (about 2 cups)*
1 *large carrot, sliced thin*
a 16-ounce can whole tomatoes, drained and chopped coarse
½ *teaspoon dried thyme, crumbled*

ACCOMPANIMENT: *freshly grated Parmesan*

In a large heavy saucepan cook leeks in oil over moderately low heat, stirring, until softened. While leeks are cooking, peel artichokes or potatoes and cut into ½-inch pieces. Add artichokes or potatoes to leeks with remaining ingredients and bring mixture to a boil. Simmer soup 20 minutes, or until vegetables are tender. *Soup may be made 1 day ahead and cooled completely, uncovered, before being chilled, covered. Reheat soup.* Season soup with salt and pepper and transfer to a thermos to keep warm.

Serve soup sprinkled with Parmesan.

Makes about 10 cups, serving 6.

Goat Cheese, Polenta, and Mushroom Tart

═══

1 recipe butter pastry dough (page 210)
½ pound mushrooms, sliced
1 stick (½ cup) unsalted butter, softened
1 cup basic polenta, cooled (page 210)
½ cup sour cream
¼ pound soft mild goat cheese
2 large eggs, beaten lightly
½ teaspoon salt
1 tablespoon small fresh thyme sprigs

Preheat oven to 375° F.

On a floured surface with a floured rolling pin roll out dough into a 15-inch round (about ⅛ inch thick) and fit into a 9-inch quiche dish. Trim overhang to ½ inch and fold toward center, pressing against side of dish. Chill shell while sautéing mushrooms.

In a skillet sauté mushrooms with salt to taste in 2 tablespoons butter over moderately high heat until golden and liquid mushrooms give off is evaporated.

Spread mushrooms in shell and bake tart in middle of oven 20 minutes.

While tart is baking, in a bowl stir together polenta, sour cream, and remaining 6 tablespoons butter until combined well. Force goat cheese through small teardrop-shaped holes of a hand grater and stir into polenta mixture with eggs and salt.

Spread polenta filling over mushrooms and scatter with thyme on top. Bake tart 35 minutes more, or until filling is puffed and golden. Cool tart slightly in dish on a rack. *Tart may be made 4 hours ahead and kept, loosely covered, at room temperature.* Serve tart warm or at room temperature.

Serves 6.

Photo below

Butter Pastry Dough

===

1½ cups all-purpose flour

1 teaspoon salt

1 stick cold unsalted butter, cut into bits

3 to 4 tablespoons ice water

In a bowl whisk together flour and salt and with a pastry blender or fingertips blend in butter until mixture resembles coarse meal. Add enough ice water, 1 tablespoon at a time, tossing with a fork to incorporate, until mixture begins to form a dough. On a floured surface smear dough in 3 or 4 forward motions with heel of hand to make dough easier to work with. Form dough into a ball and flatten to form a disk. *Chill dough, wrapped in plastic wrap, at least 1 hour and up to 3 days.*

Makes enough dough for a 9-inch tart.

Basic Polenta

1⅓ cups water

¼ teaspoon salt

⅓ cup instant polenta or cornmeal

In a heavy saucepan bring water with salt to a boil and add polenta or cornmeal in a slow stream, whisking. Cook polenta over moderately low heat (it should barely boil), stirring constantly, until very thick and pulls away from side of pan, about 15 minutes for instant polenta and about 40 minutes for cornmeal.

Makes about 1 cup.

Potato and Green Bean Salad with Citrus Miso Dressing

1½ pounds red potatoes

1½ pounds green beans or a combination of green and wax beans, trimmed and cut diagonally into 1½-inch pieces

2 tablespoons yellow miso (fermented soybean paste)*

2 tablespoons fresh lemon juice

2 tablespoons fresh orange juice

1 tablespoon vegetable oil

1 teaspoon Sherry vinegar

½ cup fresh parsley leaves, chopped

2 tablespoons minced drained bottled peperoncini (pickled Tuscan peppers)

*available at natural foods stores and some specialty foods shops

Cut potatoes into ¾-inch wedges. On a large steamer rack set over boiling water steam potatoes, covered, until just tender, about 10 minutes, and transfer to a bowl. Steam beans on rack over boiling water, covered, until just tender, about 6 minutes, and add to potatoes. *Vegetables may be steamed 1 day ahead and chilled, covered. Bring vegetables to room temperature before proceeding.*

In a large bowl whisk together *miso*, citrus juices, oil, and vinegar and add steamed vegetables, parsley, and *peperoncini*. Toss salad until combined well and season with salt.

Serves 6.

Photo on page 206

CHEWY HAZELNUT BARS

═══

FOR CRUST

    1 stick (½ cup) unsalted butter, softened

    ¼ cup packed brown sugar

    1 large egg

    ¾ cup all-purpose flour

    1 cup graham cracker crumbs (about 8
       large crackers)

    ¼ teaspoon salt

FOR TOPPING

    1 cup packed brown sugar

    2 large eggs, beaten lightly

    ¼ cup Frangelico (hazelnut-flavored liqueur)

    ¼ cup all-purpose flour

    ¾ teaspoon baking powder

    ¼ teaspoon salt

    1 cup coarsely chopped hazelnuts

    3 ounces fine-quality bittersweet chocolate
      (not unsweetened), chopped

Preheat oven to 350° F. Butter and flour a
13- by 9- by 2-inch baking pan, knocking out
excess flour.

Make crust:

In a bowl with an electric mixer beat
together butter and brown sugar until fluffy
and beat in egg until smooth. Add flour,
crumbs, and salt and beat until just combined. With floured hands press mixture onto
bottom of baking pan. Bake crust in middle of
oven until golden brown and sides begin to
pull away from pan, about 15 minutes, and
cool in pan on a rack.

Make topping:

In a bowl whisk together brown sugar,
eggs, Frangelico, flour, baking powder, and
salt and stir in nuts.

Pour topping evenly over crust and bake
in middle of oven 30 minutes, or until golden.
Cool dessert completely in pan on rack.

Run a knife around edge of pan to loosen
dessert and cut into 24 bars. In a small bowl
set over a saucepan of simmering water melt
chocolate, stirring until smooth. Drizzle
chocolate with a fork decoratively over bars
and chill bars in pan until chocolate is set,
about 10 minutes. *Bars may be made 2 days
ahead and kept in layers separated by wax
paper in an airtight container, chilled.*

Makes 24 bars.

A good novel, large towels, sunglasses, suntan lotion . . . and a cooler packed with a carefree picnic are all beach essentials. Our portable menu is an ample feast for friends to enjoy throughout the day. The chilled soup will keep you cool, two different heros and a simple but satisfying salad will keep hunger away, and luscious turnovers will satisfy all sweet urges.

CHILLED YOGURT AND SCALLION SOUP
WITH TARRAGON

MOROCCAN-SPICED CAPONATA
AND BASIL HEROS

MEDITERRANEAN TUNA HEROS

CHICK-PEA SALAD WITH
ORANGE GINGER VINAIGRETTE

RASPBERRY AND LEMON
CREAM CHEESE TURNOVERS

Simi Rosé de Cabernet Sauvignon 1996

SERVES 8

◆ Caponata heros: Caponata must be chilled at least 2 hours and up to 3 days; sandwiches may be made 6 hours ahead.

◆ Tuna heros: Filling may be made 1 day ahead; sandwiches may be made 6 hours ahead.

◆ Soup must be chilled at least 2 hours.

◆ Salad must be chilled at least 1 hour.

◆ Turnovers may be made 1 day ahead.

A DAY AT THE BEACH

CHILLED YOGURT AND SCALLION SOUP WITH TARRAGON

═══

2 cups chopped scallion including greens (about 1½ bunches)

2 tablespoons extra-virgin olive oil

8 cups chicken broth

2½ cups plain yogurt

2 large egg yolks

2 tablespoons finely chopped fresh tarragon leaves

In a small kettle cook 1¾ cups scallion in oil over moderately low heat, stirring, until softened, about 5 minutes. Add chicken broth and simmer, uncovered, 10 minutes. In a heatproof bowl whisk together yogurt and yolks and add 1 cup hot broth in a stream, whisking. Whisk yogurt mixture into scallion mixture and cook over moderately low heat, stirring, until soup registers 170° F. on an instant-read thermometer, 1 to 2 minutes. Stir in tarragon, remaining ¼ cup scallion, and salt and pepper to taste and cool completely. *Chill soup, covered, at least until ice cold, about 2 hours, and up to 1 day.*

Makes about 10 cups, serving 8.

MOROCCAN-SPICED CAPONATA AND BASIL HEROS

═══

FOR CAPONATA

2 tablespoons paprika

1 teaspoon ground cumin

½ teaspoon ground allspice

½ teaspoon cinnamon

2 medium eggplants (about 2 pounds), cut into 1-inch cubes

1 large red bell pepper, cut into ½-inch pieces

1 large yellow bell pepper, cut into ½-inch pieces

1 large onion, chopped

4 garlic cloves, chopped

2 cups water

⅓ cup fresh lemon juice

¼ cup sugar

2 medium zucchini, cut into ¾-inch cubes

2 loaves Italian or French bread (about 17 by 3½ inches each)

1 cup packed fresh basil leaves

Make caponata:

In a dry heavy kettle toast spices over moderate heat, stirring, until fragrant, about 1 minute. Stir in eggplants, bell peppers, onion, garlic, water, lemon juice, sugar, and salt and pepper to taste and simmer, covered, stirring occasionally, about 10 minutes, or until eggplant is almost tender. Stir in zucchini and simmer, uncovered, until vegetables are tender and most of liquid is evaporated, about 10 minutes. Cool *caponata* slightly and transfer to a bowl. *Chill caponata, covered, until cold, about 2 hours, and up to 3 days.*

Halve loaves horizontally with a serrated knife and make 2 large heros with *caponata* and basil. Cut each hero into 4 sandwiches and wrap each separately in plastic wrap. *Sandwiches may be made 6 hours ahead and chilled.*

Makes 8 sandwiches.

Photo below

MEDITERRANEAN TUNA HEROS

FOR FILLING

> three 6-ounce cans tuna packed in oil, drained
>
> 1 cup pitted Kalamata or other black olives, chopped coarse
>
> ½ cup drained bottled pimientos, chopped
>
> ½ cup chopped scallion
>
> ⅓ cup chopped fresh coriander leaves
>
> ¼ cup thinly sliced seeded peperoncini (pickled Tuscan peppers)
>
> ¼ cup mayonnaise
>
> 1 tablespoon fresh lemon juice
>
> 2 loaves Italian or French bread (about 17 by 3½ inches each)
>
> 4 cups shredded romaine (about 1 small head)

Make filling:

In a bowl stir together all filling ingredients until combined well but still chunky. *Filling may be made 1 day ahead and chilled, covered.*

Halve loaves horizontally with a serrated knife and make 2 large heros with filling and romaine. Cut each hero into 4 sandwiches and wrap each separately in plastic wrap. *Sandwiches may be made 6 hours ahead and chilled.*

Makes 8 sandwiches.

CHICK-PEA SALAD WITH ORANGE GINGER VINAIGRETTE

══

FOR VINAIGRETTE

    3 tablespoons fresh orange juice

    3 tablespoons white-wine vinegar

    1 garlic clove, minced

    2 teaspoons grated peeled fresh gingerroot, or to taste

    ¼ teaspoon cayenne or dried hot red pepper flakes, or to taste

    ½ cup olive oil

three 19-ounce cans chick-peas, rinsed and drained well

2 cucumbers, peeled, seeded, and chopped

2 vine-ripened tomatoes, seeded and chopped

1 small red onion, chopped

½ cup finely chopped fresh parsley leaves

Make vinaigrette:

In a bowl whisk together all vinaigrette ingredients except oil and season with salt and pepper. Add oil in a stream, whisking until emulsified.

In a large bowl toss together remaining ingredients and vinaigrette until combined well. *Chill salad, covered, at least 1 hour and up to 1 day.*

Serves 8.

RASPBERRY AND LEMON CREAM CHEESE TURNOVERS

====

3 tablespoons cornstarch

½ cup sugar plus additional for sprinkling turnovers

½ cup fresh lemon juice

¼ cup water

1 teaspoon finely grated fresh lemon zest

¾ cup cream cheese (about 6 ounces), softened

2 frozen puff pastry sheets (a 17¼-ounce package), thawed

about 1 cup raspberries

an egg wash made by beating 1 large egg with 1 teaspoon water

In a small saucepan whisk together cornstarch and ½ cup sugar and whisk in lemon juice, water, and zest until combined. Bring mixture to a boil, whisking, and simmer, whisking, 1 minute. Transfer lemon mixture to a bowl and whisk in cream cheese until smooth. Cool lemon cream cheese.

Preheat oven to 425° F.

On a lightly floured surface roll out each pastry sheet into a 12-inch square and cut each square into four 6-inch squares. Mound about 3 tablespoons lemon cream cheese in center of each square and top with 1 heaping tablespoon raspberries. Brush edges of each square with water and fold squares in half to form triangles, pressing edges together firmly. Crimp edges with tines of a fork to seal well. Arrange turnovers on 2 baking sheets and brush tops with egg wash. With a sharp knife cut several slits in top of each turnover to form steam vents and sprinkle with additional sugar.

Bake turnovers in middle and upper thirds of oven, switching position of sheets halfway through baking, 12 to 15 minutes, or until puffed and golden. *Turnovers may be made 1 day ahead and cooled completely before being kept in one layer in an airtight container.* Serve turnovers warm or at room temperature.

Makes 8 turnovers.

A fter a hike or bird-watching expedition, or, for that matter, any warm-weather outing, spread out a few tartan blankets in a shady meadow for our old-fashioned picnic. It's packed with favorites, including a potato salad just like the one you loved as a kid. Shortcakes with berries are an impressive finale that require some last-minute assembly. Remember to bring along a serrated knife for splitting the ginger shortcakes, and serving spoons for scooping up the mixed berries with their juices and the tangy whipped cream yogurt topping.

◆ Potato salad may be made 1 day ahead.

◆ Shortcakes with berries: Berries must macerate at least 4 hours and up to 1 day; shortcakes may be baked 4 hours ahead; cream topping may be made 4 hours ahead.

◆ Sandwiches may be made 6 hours ahead.

LUNCH IN THE MEADOW

Salami, Prosciutto, Havarti, and Slaw Sandwiches

⅓ cup olive oil

2 tablespoons red-wine vinegar

1 teaspoon dried oregano, crumbled

2 cups shredded cabbage

1 red bell pepper, sliced into very thin strips

½ cup finely chopped dill pickle

8 hard kaiser rolls

½ cup mayonnaise

¾ pound thinly sliced hard salami

½ pound thinly sliced prosciutto

¾ pound Havarti cheese with dill, sliced thin

In a small bowl whisk together oil, vinegar, oregano, and salt and pepper to taste. Add cabbage, bell pepper, and pickle and toss until combined.

Halve rolls horizontally with a serrated knife, cutting almost but not all the way through, and make sandwiches with mayonnaise, salami, prosciutto, Havarti, and slaw. *Sandwiches may be made 6 hours ahead and chilled, wrapped in plastic wrap.*

Makes 8 sandwiches.

Old-Fashioned Potato Salad

5 pounds boiling potatoes

1 tablespoon red-wine vinegar

5 boiled large eggs, chopped

2 green bell peppers, chopped fine

1 cup thinly sliced onion (about 1 medium)

1 cup mayonnaise

½ cup finely chopped dill pickle or sweet pickles

½ cup chopped fresh parsley leaves

¼ cup sour cream

¼ cup yellow mustard

1 teaspoon paprika

In a kettle cover potatoes with cold salted water by 1 inch and simmer just until tender, about 20 minutes. In a colander drain potatoes and rinse under cold water until just cool enough to handle. Peel potatoes and cut into bite-size pieces.

In a large bowl toss warm potatoes with vinegar and cool completely. Toss potatoes with remaining ingredients and salt and pepper to taste until combined well. *Salad may be made 1 day ahead and chilled, covered.* Serve potato salad chilled or at room temperature.

Serves 8.

Ginger Shortcakes
with Berries
in Vanilla Syrup

===

FOR BERRY MIXTURE

1 vanilla bean

1 quart blackberries, picked over

1 quart raspberries, picked over

1 quart blueberries, picked over

¾ cup granulated sugar

FOR SHORTCAKES

3 cups all-purpose flour

⅓ cup plus 1 tablespoon granulated sugar

1 tablespoon baking powder

¾ teaspoon baking soda

¾ teaspoon salt

1½ sticks cold unsalted butter, cut into bits

2 tablespoons finely grated peeled fresh gingerroot

1½ teaspoons finely grated fresh orange zest

1 cup sour cream

1 cup milk

FOR YOGURT CREAM

1 cup well-chilled heavy cream

2 tablespoons confectioners' sugar

¼ cup plain yogurt

Make berry mixture:

Split vanilla bean lengthwise and with a knife scrape seeds into a large bowl or sealable container, reserving pod for another use. Add 2 cups of each berry and ¾ cup sugar and with a potato masher crush berries lightly. *Macerate berries, covered, at room temperature*

4 hours. Fold in remaining whole berries. Berry mixture may be made 1 day ahead and chilled, covered. Bring mixture to room temperature before serving.

Make shortcakes:

Preheat oven to 425° F. and lightly butter 2 baking sheets.

In a large bowl whisk together flour, ⅓ cup sugar, baking powder, baking soda, and salt and with your fingertips or a pastry blender blend in butter until mixture resembles coarse meal. In a small bowl whisk together gingerroot, zest, sour cream, and milk and add to flour mixture, stirring until a soft, sticky dough just forms. Drop dough in 10 mounds about 1 inch apart onto baking sheets and sprinkle tops with remaining tablespoon sugar.

Bake shortcakes in upper and lower thirds of oven, switching position of sheets halfway through baking, 12 to 15 minutes, or until pale golden. Transfer shortcakes to a rack and cool. *Shortcakes may be made 4 hours ahead and kept in airtight containers at room temperature.*

Make yogurt cream:

In a large bowl beat cream with confectioners' sugar until it holds soft peaks and beat in yogurt. Transfer yogurt cream to a sealable container. *Yogurt cream may be made 4 hours ahead and chilled, covered. Stir cream gently before serving.*

Halve shortcakes horizontally with a serrated knife and serve with berry mixture and yogurt cream.

Serves 8.

Photo on page 218

Doughnuts and extra-rich hot chocolate will warm your guests for hours of ice-skating. And, when you come back from the rink, our abundant chili supper will be ready in no time, since every-thing, except the salad dressing, can be made the day before. You can even wash and dry the salad greens and quarter the cherry tomatoes for the salad a day ahead.

RICH HOT CHOCOLATE

CHOCOLATE DOUGHNUTS

RAISED DOUGHNUTS

MAPLE BARS

CHEESE AND CORN TORTILLA WEDGES

SHREDDED BEEF AND CHICKEN CHILI

RICE AND BEANS

TOSSED SALAD
WITH AVOCADO DRESSING

APPLE PINEAPPLE CRISP

Clos du Bois
Sonoma County Merlot 1994

SERVES 12

◆ Chili may be made 4 days ahead.

◆ Rice and beans may be made 2 days ahead.

◆ Crisp may be baked 1 day ahead.

◆ Hot chocolate may be made 1 day ahead.

◆ Doughnuts: Dough for the raised dough-nuts and maple bars may be prepared the night before; all three doughnuts may be fried 6 hours ahead.

ICE SKATING PARTY

RICH HOT CHOCOLATE

9¾ cups milk

1½ cups heavy cream

1½ tablespoons vanilla

18 ounces fine-quality bittersweet chocolate
(not unsweetened), chopped fine

GARNISH: *miniature marshmallows*

In a 6- to 7-quart heavy kettle bring milk, cream, vanilla, and a pinch salt just to a boil over moderate heat. In a heatproof bowl whisk together chocolate and about 2 cups hot milk mixture until smooth. Whisk chocolate mixture into remaining milk mixture and simmer, whisking, 2 minutes. *Hot chocolate may be made 1 day ahead and cooled to room temperature before being chilled, covered. Reheat hot chocolate, whisking, before serving.*

Divide hot chocolate among mugs and top with marshmallows.

Makes about 14 cups, serving 12.

Photo above

CHOCOLATE DOUGHNUTS

⅓ cup vegetable shortening, melted and
cooled

⅔ cup granulated sugar

2 large eggs

¾ cup well-shaken buttermilk

3 cups all-purpose flour

½ cup unsweetened cocoa powder

2 teaspoons baking powder

1 teaspoon baking soda

1 teaspoon salt

vegetable oil for deep-frying

FOR GLAZE

1 ounce unsweetened chocolate

¼ cup water

2 cups confectioners' sugar

In a large bowl stir together shortening, sugar, and eggs and stir in buttermilk until combined well. Onto buttermilk mixture sift together flour, cocoa powder, baking powder, baking soda, and salt and stir just until a dough forms. On a lightly floured surface knead dough about 6 times, or until smooth. Pat and roll out dough ½ inch thick and with a floured 2½-inch doughnut cutter cut out doughnuts, transferring them and holes to a sheet of wax paper. Knead scraps together gently and make more doughnuts in same manner.

In a deep kettle heat 2 inches oil over moderately high heat to 375° F. on a deep-fat thermometer. Working in batches, drop 3 or 4 doughnuts and holes into oil and fry, turning them as they rise to surface and 3 or 4 more times, until a darker brown, 2 to 3 minutes. Transfer doughnuts and holes as fried with a slotted spoon to paper towels to drain.

Make glaze:

In a metal bowl set over a saucepan of simmering water melt chocolate with ¼ cup water, stirring, and remove bowl from heat. Whisk in confectioners' sugar until smooth.

While doughnuts are still warm, dip tops in glaze and dry doughnuts on racks 5 minutes. *Doughnuts may be made 6 hours ahead and kept in an airtight container.*

Makes about 20 doughnuts.

Photo on page 222

RAISED DOUGHNUTS

==

½ cup warm milk (105° to 115° F.)
½ cup warm water (105° to 115° F.)
a ¼-ounce package active dry yeast
½ cup granulated sugar
¾ stick unsalted butter, softened
1 teaspoon salt
½ teaspoon freshly grated nutmeg
3¼ to 3½ cups all-purpose flour
vegetable oil for deep-frying
sugar glaze or cinnamon sugar (page 226)

In a large bowl stir together milk, water, and yeast and let stand until foamy, about 5 minutes. Add sugar and butter and whisk until combined well (lumps of butter will remain).

Add salt, nutmeg, and 2 cups flour and beat until a smooth batter forms. Stir in 1¼ cups flour to form a soft but manageable dough and on a lightly floured surface knead dough 2 minutes. Let dough stand 10 minutes. Continue to knead dough, adding enough of remaining ¼ cup flour to keep dough from sticking. Transfer dough to an oiled bowl, turning to coat. *Let dough rise, covered, in a warm place until doubled in bulk, about 1½ hours. (Alternatively, let dough rise, covered and chilled, overnight.)*

On floured surface roll out dough ½ inch thick and with a floured 2½-inch doughnut cutter cut out doughnuts, transferring them and holes to a sheet of wax paper. Knead scraps together gently and make more doughnuts in same manner. *Let doughnuts and holes rise, covered loosely with wax paper, in a warm place until almost doubled in bulk, about 1 hour.*

In a deep kettle heat 2 inches oil over moderately high heat to 375° F. on a deep-fat thermometer. Working in batches, drop 3 or 4 doughnuts and holes into oil and fry, turning them as they rise to surface and 3 or 4 more times, until golden, 2 to 3 minutes. Transfer doughnuts and holes as fried with a slotted spoon to paper towels to drain.

While doughnuts are still warm, dip tops in glaze or toss doughnuts with cinnamon sugar. Transfer doughnuts to racks and dry 5 minutes. *Doughnuts may be made 6 hours ahead and kept in an airtight container at room temperature.*

Makes about 20 doughnuts.

Photo on page 222

SUGAR GLAZE

2 cups confectioners' sugar

⅓ cup water

1 teaspoon vanilla

In a small bowl whisk together all ingredients and a pinch salt until smooth.

Makes about ⅔ cup.

CINNAMON SUGAR

1 cup sugar

2 teaspoons cinnamon

In a bowl stir together sugar and cinnamon.

Makes about 1 cup.

MAPLE BARS

a ¼-ounce package (2½ teaspoons) active dry yeast

⅔ cup warm milk (105° to 115° F.)

2 large eggs

¾ stick (6 tablespoons) unsalted butter, softened

⅓ cup granulated sugar

1 teaspoon vanilla

½ teaspoon freshly grated nutmeg

½ teaspoon salt

3¼ to 3¾ cups all-purpose flour

vegetable oil for deep-frying

FOR GLAZE

2 cups confectioners' sugar

about ½ cup maple syrup

In a large bowl sprinkle yeast over milk and let stand until foamy, about 5 minutes. Add eggs, butter, sugar, vanilla, nutmeg, and salt and whisk until combined well (lumps of butter will remain). Add 2 cups flour and beat until batter is smooth. Stir in enough of remaining 1¾ cups flour to form a soft but manageable dough and on a lightly floured surface knead dough 2 minutes. Let dough stand 10 minutes. Knead dough 5 minutes more, or until smooth and elastic, and transfer to an oiled bowl, turning to coat. *Let dough rise, covered, in a warm place until doubled in bulk, about 1½ hours. (Alternatively, let dough rise, covered and chilled, overnight.)*

On floured surface roll out dough into a ½-inch-thick square and cut into 4- by 2-inch rectangles. Transfer rectangles to a sheet of wax paper and let rise, covered loosely with wax paper, in a warm place until almost doubled in bulk, about 40 minutes.

In a deep kettle heat 2 inches oil over moderately high heat to 375° F. on a deep-fat thermometer. Working in batches, drop 3 or 4 rectangles into oil and fry, turning them as they rise to surface and 3 or 4 more times, until golden brown, 2 to 3 minutes. Transfer maple bars as fried with a slotted spoon to paper towels to drain.

Make glaze:

In a small bowl whisk together confectioners' sugar and ½ cup maple syrup, adding a little more syrup if necessary to reach a smooth spreading consistency.

While maple bars are still warm, spread top of each bar with about 1 tablespoon glaze and dry on racks 5 minutes. *Bars may be made 6 hours ahead and kept in an airtight container at room temperature.*

Makes about 16 bars.

Photo on page 222

TORTILLA WEDGES

3 cups fresh or thawed frozen corn
1 cup finely chopped roasted red bell pepper
1 cup finely chopped red onion
1 cup packed fresh coriander sprigs, chopped
about 1 cup plus 1½ tablespoons vegetable oil
twenty-four 6- to 7-inch corn tortillas*
6 cups grated pepper jack cheese
¼ teaspoon cayenne

*available at supermarkets and by mail (page 231)

Preheat oven to 450° F.

In a bowl toss together corn, roasted pepper, onion, and coriander. In a 10-inch heavy skillet heat ½ cup oil over moderate heat until hot but not smoking and fry tortillas, 1 at a time, just until softened, 3 to 5 seconds (do not let tortillas crisp), adding ½ cup additional oil as needed. Transfer tortillas as softened to paper towels with a slotted spatula, blotting up excess oil with additional paper towels. On each of 2 large heavy baking sheets arrange 3 tortillas in one layer. Top each tortilla with about ⅓ cup corn mixture and ⅓ cup cheese and top with a second tortilla. Make 2 more layers on each tortilla in same manner with remaining corn mixture, cheese, and tortillas, gently pressing each layer down and ending with a fourth tortilla on top of each cake.

In a bowl stir together cayenne and remaining 1½ tablespoons oil and brush over top of each cake. Bake cakes until golden, about 12 minutes, and cut into wedges.

Serves 12.

SHREDDED BEEF AND CHICKEN CHILI

==

¼ pound salt pork, cut into ¼-inch dice

3 large onions, chopped coarse

2 green bell peppers, chopped

8 garlic cloves, minced

½ cup chili powder, or to taste

5 pounds boneless beef chuck, cut into
    4 pieces

3 pounds skinless chicken thighs

5 cups water

3 cups beef broth

a 28- to 32-ounce can whole tomatoes,
    chopped, including juice

3 pickled whole jalapeño chilies, stems
    discarded and chilies chopped (include
    some seeds for hotter chili)

1 tablespoon dried oregano, crumbled

2 teaspoons salt, or to taste

2 tablespoons cornmeal

ACCOMPANIMENTS:

rice and beans (recipe follows)

sour cream

chopped fresh coriander sprigs

In a large heavy kettle cook salt pork over moderately low heat, stirring, until crisp and browned. Add onions, bell peppers, and garlic and cook, stirring, until onions are softened. Add chili powder and cook, stirring, 30 seconds. Add beef, chicken, water, broth, tomatoes with juice, *jalapeños*, oregano, and salt and simmer, partially covered, until beef is fork-tender, 2 to 2½ hours. Transfer beef and chicken with a slotted spoon to a large bowl and skim fat from braising liquid in kettle. When cool enough to handle shred meats, discarding bones, and return to kettle. Stir in cornmeal and simmer chili, stirring occasionally, 5 minutes, or until slightly thickened. *Chili may be made 4 days ahead and cooled completely, uncovered, before being chilled, covered. Reheat chili before serving.*

Serve chili over rice and beans and top with sour cream and coriander.

Serves 12.

RICE AND BEANS

==

4½ cups water

2½ cups long-grain white rice

1½ teaspoons salt

a 19-ounce can black or kidney beans,
    rinsed and drained

In a large heavy saucepan with a tight-fitting lid stir together water, rice, and salt and boil, uncovered, without stirring, until surface is covered with steam holes and grains on top appear dry, 6 to 8 minutes. Reduce heat to very low and cook rice, covered, 15 minutes, or until water is absorbed and rice is tender. Remove pan from heat and let rice stand, covered, 5 minutes. Fluff rice with a fork and stir in beans. *Rice and beans may be made 2 days ahead and cooled completely, uncovered, before being chilled, covered. Reheat rice and beans in a large colander covered with a dampened paper towel and set over a large saucepan of boiling water.*

Serves 12.

TOSSED SALAD WITH AVOCADO DRESSING

1 ripe California avocado

½ cup sour cream

3 tablespoons fresh lemon juice

3 tablespoons olive oil

1 teaspoon honey

1 garlic clove, chopped

1 teaspoon bottled jalapeño sauce

¼ teaspoon ground cumin

¼ teaspoon salt

4 to 6 tablespoons cold water

16 cups torn mixed salad greens

1 pint vine-ripened cherry tomatoes, quartered

¾ pound radishes (about 2 cups), sliced thin

⅔ cup hulled pumpkin seeds or roasted hulled sunflower seeds

Halve, pit, and peel avocado. Chop avocado and transfer half to a blender, reserving other half in a large bowl for salad. To avocado in blender add sour cream, lemon juice, oil, honey, garlic, hot sauce, cumin, and salt and blend, adding enough water to reach desired consistency, until smooth.

In large bowl gently toss together reserved avocado, remaining ingredients, and dressing until combined.

Serves 12.

APPLE PINEAPPLE CRISP

2 pounds tart apples such as Cortland, Northern Spy, or Jonathan (about 4 large)

three 8-ounce cans pineapple chunks, drained

2 cups old-fashioned rolled oats

1 cup chopped macadamia nuts or almonds

¾ cup packed brown sugar

¾ cup granulated sugar

1 stick (½ cup) cold unsalted butter, cut into bits

½ cup all-purpose flour

¼ cup fresh lemon juice

1 teaspoon cinnamon

1 teaspoon ground ginger

¼ teaspoon freshly grated nutmeg

¾ teaspoon salt

ACCOMPANIMENT: *vanilla frozen yogurt or whipped cream*

Preheat oven to 350° F. and butter a 13- by 9-inch glass baking dish.

Peel and core apples. Slice apples ¼-inch thick and in baking dish toss with pineapple chunks. In a bowl combine remaining ingredients and blend with fingers until crumbly. Sprinkle topping over fruit and bake in middle of oven 30 to 40 minutes, or until fruit is bubbling and topping is crisp. *Crisp may be made 1 day ahead and cooled completely before being kept, covered, at room temperature. Reheat crisp in a preheated 350° F. oven until hot, about 15 minutes.* Serve crisp warm with frozen yogurt or whipped cream.

Serves 12.

MAIL ORDER SOURCES

ADRIANA'S CARAVAN, Brooklyn, NY
tel. (800) 316-0820 or (212) 436-8565
*for chipotle chilies, fresh lemongrass, dried morels, polenta rolls,
and just about any other ethnic or specialty ingredient*

D'ARTAGNAN, Jersey City, NJ
tel. (800) 327-8246 or (201) 792-0748
for pheasants, fresh game, specialty meats

DEAN & DELUCA CATALOG AND STORE,
New York, NY
tel. (800) 221-7714 for catalog; (212) 226-6800 for store
*for crystallized violets, chipotle chilies, dried morels, pheasants,
and many other specialty foods (items not available through catalog
may be available by mail from the store)*

DELFTREE FARM, North Adams, MA
tel. (800) 243-3742 or (413) 664-4907;
fax (413) 664-4908
*for dried morels, fresh and dried organic shiitakes and dried wild
mushrooms*

GOURMET MUSHROOMS, Sebastopol, CA
tel. (707) 823-1743; fax (707) 823-1507
for dried morels, fresh and dried cultivated and wild mushrooms

JOE'S STONE CRAB RESTAURANT, Miami Beach, FL
tel. (800) 780-CRAB or (305) 673-9035;
fax (800) 434-2529
*for ready-to-eat cooked stone crab claws (shipped with mallet and
cutting board)*

KALUSTYAN'S, New York, NY
tel. (212) 685-3451; fax (212) 683-8458
for East and West Indian, Middle Eastern, and Asian ingredients

KITCHEN, New York, NY
tel. (212) 243-4433
*for canned chipotle chilies in adobo sauce, dried chilies, and some
other Latino ingredients*

MARIA AND RICARDO'S TORTILLA FACTORY,
Jamaica Plain, MA
tel. (800) 881-7040 or (617) 524-6107
for flour, corn, and flavored tortillas

MEADOWSWEETS, Middleburgh, NY
tel. (888) 827-6477
for crystallized flowers such as pansies, primroses, and violas

NEW YORK CAKE & BAKING DISTRIBUTORS,
New York, NY
tel. (800) 942-2539 or (212) 675-2253;
fax (212) 675-7099
*for dried egg whites such as Just Whites, if egg safety is a problem
in your area; crystallized violets, and other specialty confection and
baking ingredients*

PENZEY'S, LTD, Waukesha, WI
tel. (414) 574-0277; fax (414) 574-0278
for spices, dried herbs

PHILLIPS MUSHROOM PLACE, Kennett Square, PA
tel. (800) 243-8644 or (610) 388-6082;
fax (610) 388-3985
for dried morels, fresh and dried cultivated mushrooms

TODARO BROTHERS, New York, NY
tel. (212) 679-7766 or (212) 532-0633;
fax (212) 689-1679
for polenta rolls and Italian and European imported ingredients

UWAJIMAYA, Seattle, WA
tel. (800) 889-1928 or (206) 624-6248;
fax (206) 624-6915
for fresh lemongrass and other Asian ingredients

TABLE SETTING ACKNOWLEDGMENTS

Any items in the photographs not credited are privately owned.
All addresses are in New York City unless otherwise indicated.

FRONT JACKET

Coriander Lime Shrimp; Prosciutto-Wrapped Asparagus; Roasted Sweet Potato Bites; Indonesian Peanut Dip with Crudités; Stone Crab Claws with Parsley Horseradish Sauce: "Luster" porcelain dinner/salad plates and bowl—Swid Powell. For stores call (800) 808-SWID. Art Deco silver-plate caviar server, circa 1930; French porcelain shell dish, circa 1880—James II Galleries, Ltd., 11 East 57th Street. Ceramic footbath; crystal compote; metal folding table—William-Wayne, 850 Lexington Avenue. Luster jug, circa 1830; mother-of-pearl and silver-plate forks, Sheffield, 1880 (from a 24-piece dessert set)—S. Wyler, 941 Lexington Avenue. "Vega" Martini glasses; "Lalande" crystal Champagne flutes—Baccarat, 625 Madison Avenue. Beaded organdy cocktail napkins—Dransfield and Ross. For stores call (212) 741-7278. French 1940's-style sycamore and brass-trimmed dining table with inlaid center—Newel Art Galleries, 425 East 53rd Street.

BACK JACKET

Grapefruit Rum Coolers: See Table Setting credits for **LUNCH AFLOAT.**

Roasted Butternut Squash, Rosemary, and Garlic Lasagne: See Table Setting credits for **CONTEMPORARY VEGETARIAN SUPPER.**

Ginger Shortcakes with Berries in Vanilla Syrup: See Table Setting credits for **LUNCH IN THE MEADOW.**

HALF-TITLE PAGE

Place Setting (page 1): Puiforcat "Variations Green" porcelain presentation plates. For stores call (800) 993-2580. "Feather Edge" sterling flatware—James Robinson, 480 Park Avenue. Beaded linen/cotton place mats and napkins—Dransfield and Ross. For stores call (212) 741-7278.

FRONTISPIECE

Table Setting (pages 2 and 3): Gien "Tamarin" faience plates—Baccarat, 625 Madison Avenue. "Bamboo" sterling flatware—Tiffany & Company, 727 Fifth Avenue. "Laurel Green" wineglasses and water goblets—for stores call Sasaki (212) 686-5080. "Crespo Lino" linen and cotton napkins—for stores call Anichini (800) 553-5309. Wooden napkin rings—ABC Carpet & Home, 888 Broadway. Glass vase—Pottery Barn. For stores call (800) 922-5507. "Palma" cotton fabric (available through decorator)—Brunschwig & Fils, 979 Third Avenue. "Wickerwork" cotton fabric (available through decorator)—F. Schumacher & Co., 939 Third Avenue. "Snowflake" wrought-iron chairs—Lexington Furniture Industries, (800) 544-4694. Handmade mahogany planter's chairs with canvas seats—Estate Mount Washington Plantation, (809) 772-1026. Photographed at the Estate Mount Washington Plantation, Frederiksted, Saint Croix.

TABLE OF CONTENTS

Dining Room Table Setting (page 6, top): "Camelot" porcelain soup plates designed by Robert Lee Morris for Swid Powell; silver-plate trays (under soup plates) and candlesticks designed by Richard Meier for Swid Powell—Bloomingdale's, 1000 Third Avenue. "Winslow" sterling flatware by Kirk Stieff—Fortunoff, 681 Fifth Avenue. Water goblets and wineglasses; crystal torch—Tiffany & Company, 727 Fifth Avenue. Linen napkins—Barneys New York, Seventh Avenue and Seventeenth Street. "Turquoise Stars" cotton and rayon fabric from the National Trust for Historic Preservation—F. Schumacher & Co., 939 Third Avenue. Steel and brass chairs; Art Deco steel and marble table—Newel Art Galleries, Inc., 425 East 53rd Street. Flowers—Zezé, 398 East 52nd Street.

Kitchen Table Setting (page 6, bottom): "Basique" earthenware plates by Jars—Marel, (516) 466-3118. Brass chargers—Crate & Barrel. For stores call (800) 323-5461. "Claridge" flatware by Scof—Brodean, 338 Columbus Avenue. "Provence" wineglasses (water)—Baccarat, 625 Madison Avenue. Flowerpot and saucer—Takashimaya, 693 Fifth Avenue. Flowers—Paul Bott Beautiful Flowers, 1305 Madison Avenue.

Garden Table Setting (page 7, top): See Table Setting credits for GARDEN PARTIES OPENER.

Getaways Picnic (page 7, bottom): See Table Setting credits for A DAY AT THE BEACH.

INTRODUCTION

Table Setting (page 8): Blue glass dinner plates and salad plates by Izabel Lam—The L • S Collection, 469 West Broadway. "Clipper" porcelain dinner plates (flag border) by Richard Ginori—Hoagland's, 175 Greenwich Avenue, Greenwich, CT, (203) 869-2127. "Orvieto" flatware—Williams-Sonoma. For stores call (800) 541-2233. Yellow-rimmed tumblers; white, blue, and yellow napkins—Wolfman • Gold & Good Company, 117 Mercer Street. Wire basket—Crate & Barrel. For stores call (800) 323-5461. Ian Mankin pillow fabrics—Coconut Company, 131 Greene Street.

DINING ROOM PARTIES

DINING ROOM OPENER

Table Setting (page 10): See Table Setting credits for FRONT JACKET.

AN INTIMATE NEW YEAR'S EVE

Chocolate Profiteroles (page 12): "Vulcain" porcelain dessert plate—Bernardaud, 499 Park Avenue.

Braised Pheasant with Red Cabbage Wild Rice (page 14): Royal Worcester "Gold Feather" fine bone-china service plate. For stores call (609) 866-2900. Puiforcat "Royal" sterling dinner fork—Baccarat, 625 Madison Avenue.

SUNDAY BISTRO LUNCH

Fresh Pea Soup (page 18): "Baguette" French silver-plate flatware by Chambly—Wolfman • Gold &

Good Company, 117 Mercer Street. Cotton fabric for napkins—Pierre Deux, 870 Madison Avenue. Flower arrangement—Castle & Pierpont, 1441 York Avenue. Nineteenth-century French pine bistro tabletop on modern iron and brass base—Howard Kaplan Antiques, 827 Broadway.

Chocolate Custards and Chocolate Macaroons (page 23): Kirk-Stieff "Mayflower" sterling demitasse spoons—Cardel Ltd., 621 Madison Avenue.

AUTUMN HARVEST FEAST

Date Pecan Pumpkin Squares; Nutmeg Ice Cream; Bourbon Burnt Sugar Sauce (page 24): English creamware lustre dessert plates (from a dessert service for 10), circa 1810; glass pitcher, circa 1860; oak and silver-plate tray, circa 1880—James II Galleries, Ltd., 11 East 57th Street. Pressed-glass bowl (lid not shown), circa 1840—Ages Past Antiques, 450 East 78th Street.

Pork Tenderloin and Spinach Roulades (page 26): "Pergamon" bone-china platter—Villeroy & Boch Creation, 974 Madison Avenue.

Table Setting (page 27): Gien faience dinner plates and salad plates—Baccarat, 625 Madison Avenue. "Harbor" stainless-steel flatware. For stores call Ralph Lauren Collection, (212) 624-8700. Wineglasses—Simon Pearce, 500 Park Avenue at 59th Street. Cotton napkins; short wrought-iron candlestick—Pier One Imports. For stores call (800) 245-4595. Tall wrought-iron candlesticks with crystal drops designed by Cyril Doudeau. For stores call Paradigm Exclusives, (212) 629-3955. Dried-flower arrangement—Zezé, 398 East 52nd Street.

A WELCOMING DINNER

Roasted Vegetable Napoleon (page 30): All items in photograph are privately owned.

Lemon Rosemary Custard Cakes (page 35): All items in photograph are privately owned.

SPICE UP YOUR WINTER DINNER

Coriander-Honey Chicken with Sweet-and-Sour Peanut Sauce (page 36): Bristol polychrome delft charger, circa 1750; Neale pottery sauce tureen, circa 1790, both from Bardith Ltd., 901 Madison Avenue. English silver-plate serving fork and spoon, circa 1860, from James II Galleries, Ltd., 11 East 57th Street.

Table Setting (page 41): All items in photograph are privately owned.

TWO-PIE COUNTRY DINNER

Cranberry Maple Pear Pie; Pecan Pumpkin Pie (page 42): Spode china dessert plates (from a set of 8), circa 1820—James II Galleries, Ltd., 11 East 57th Street. Handmade tassel from Alberto Pirini, Borgo Ognissanti, 22, Florence, Italy.

PACIFIC RIM DINNER

Ginger Scallops with Stir-Fried Broccoli Rabe (page 50): Laminated recycled-paper place mats designed by Catriona Stewart. For stores call Sphere Management, (212) 362-3782.

Table Setting (page 52): Flowers—Zezé, 398 East 52nd Street. Harry Lauder Stick Branches—SKH Floral Manufacturing, (717) 898-6076.

Coconut Crème Brûlée (page 55): All items in photograph are privately owned.

A SPIRITED HOLIDAY DINNER

Chocolate Grappa Cake; Honey-Grappa Compote (page 56): Crystal dessert plate—Lalique, 680 Madison Avenue. "Faneuil" sterling spoon; crystal cake stand; crystal bowl—Tiffany & Co., 727 Fifth Avenue. Crystal glasses, circa 1850 (from a set of 6); etched crystal decanters, circa 1870—Kentshire Galleries, 37 East 12th Street.

Mantelpiece (page 59): English silver-plate candelabra, circa 1880 (from a set including 4 candlesticks)—S. Wyler, 941 Lexington Avenue.

AN ELEGANT COCKTAIL PARTY

Hors d'Oeuvres Assortment (page 62): Vintage three-tiered silver-plate stand with porcelain plates—Kentshire Gallery at Bergdorf Goodman, 754 Fifth Avenue. "Pavillon" crystal wineglasses—Baccarat, 625 Madison Avenue.

Curried Scallop Canapés; Walnut Salad in Endive (page 65): Black hors d'oeuvre plates—William-Wayne & Co., 850 Lexington Avenue. Vintage silver-plate cocktail shaker—Vito Giallo, 222 East 83rd Street. Vintage English silver-plate gallery

tray—Kentshire Gallery at Bergdorf Goodman, 754 Fifth Avenue.

Brie Baked en Croûte (page 66): Philippe Deshoulieres "Fleur de Lis" porcelain cake plate; French stainless-steel pie server—Avventura, 463 Amsterdam Avenue.

KITCHEN PARTIES

KITCHEN OPENER

Kitchen Setting (page 70): no credits.

A WARMING RUSTIC SUPPER

Butternut Squash Risotto (page 72): Ceramic plates and bowl by Christiane Perrochon; linen towel by Primrose Bordier—Bergdorf Goodman, 754 Fifth Avenue. French acrylic and stainless-steel flatware—William-Wayne & Co., 850 Lexington Avenue.

A PROVENÇAL DINNER

Seafood Stew (page 76): All items in photograph are privately owned.

Herbs (page 79): All items in photograph are privately owned.

PASTA EN CUCINA SUPPER

Spaghetti with Eggplant and Tomato Sauce (page 80): "Giada" majolica dinner plates—Cottura, 7215 Melrose Avenue, Los Angeles, CA 90046.

ELECTION NIGHT DINNER

Chicken Potpie with Chive Mashed Potatoes (page 84): Belgian porcelain baking dish—Bridge Kitchenware Corp., 212 East 52nd Street. Ceramic dinner plates—Pottery Barn. For stores call (800) 922-5507. Earthenware pitcher by Eigen Arts—Gardens, 1818 West 35th Street, Austin, TX 78703, (512) 451-5490. Cotton rug (on table)—Crate & Barrel. For stores call (800) 323-5461.

Apple Pie (page 89)—"Stars & Stripes" cotton fabric (available through decorator)—Grey Watkins Ltd., 979 Third Avenue. "Classic Ticking" cotton fabric—Waverly, (800) 423-5881.

A Lazy Morning Breakfast

Buttermilk Waffles; Apple and Dried-Fruit Compote (page 90): Le Creuset enameled cast-iron saucepan (lid not shown)—Bloomingdale's, 1000 Third Avenue. "Belgian Waffler" by Vitantonio—Zabar's, 2245 Broadway. "Bondoni" clock—M & Co Labs, 225 Lafayette Street, suite 904, (212) 343-2408.

Buffet setting (page 93): "Poynter" teapot, sugar, and creamer by Recollections—The Victoria & Albert Museum Gift Shop, South Kensington, London SW7 2RL, England. Twig tray—Gordon Foster, 1322 Third Avenue. Flowers—Zezé, 398 East 52nd Street. "Madeline" hand-carved and hand-painted buffet from The Farmhouse Collection (available through decorator)—Circa David Barett, Ltd., 232 East 59th Street. "Log Cabin" wool challis quilt, circa 1880 (84 by 82 inches)—Thos. K. Woodard American Antiques and Quilts, 506 East 74th Street.

Festive Weekend Dinner

Black Bean Tart with Chili Crust (page 94): All items in photograph are privately owned.

Patio Setting (page 98): "Cordoba" recycled glass—Global Guzzini, 2465 Coral Street, Vista, CA 92083, (619) 598-0188.

Fresh from the Garden Lunch

Farm Stand (pages 100 and 104): All items in photograph are privately owned.

Back Yard Setting (page 102): Antique watering can—Wolfman • Gold & Good Company, 117 Mercer Street.

Fried Zucchini Blossoms and Bell Pepper Rings (page 103): Angela Cummings "Blue Fishnet" porcelain dinner and salad plates for Arita—Bergdorf Goodman, 754 Fifth Avenue. Wineglasses—Pottery Barn. For stores call (800) 922-5507. "Tropicana Yellow" cotton fabric (available through decorators and architects)—China Seas, Inc., 21 East 4th Street.

Brunch before a Country Stroll

Onion and Bell Pepper Strata with Fresh Tomato Salsa; White Sangría (page 106): "Classico" plates by Cyclamen Studio. For stores call (510) 843-4691. Kappa shell plates—Bergdorf Goodman, 754 Fifth Avenue. "Madeline" flatware—Pottery Barn. For stores call (800) 922-5507. "Lyra" crystal wineglasses—Baccarat, 625 Madison Avenue. Linen and raffia napkins. For stores call Archipelago, (212) 334-9460. "Symphony" crystal pitcher by Orrefors—Galleri Orrefors Kosta Boda, 58 East 57th Street.

Contemporary Vegetarian Supper

Roasted Butternut Squash, Rosemary, and Garlic Lasagne (page 110): French porcelain baking dish—Gracious Home, 1220 Third Avenue. "Acadia" stoneware salad plate; "Brighton" stainless-steel flatware; "Acadia" sculptured wineglass—Pfaltzgraff. For stores call (800) 999-2811.

Mediterranean Hors d' Oeuvres Buffet

Spinach Phyllo Pizza (page 114): All items in photograph are privately owned.

Lunch before the Playoffs

Black-Eyed Pea and Ham Stew (page 120): English ironstone tureen and ladle, circa 1850—Vito Giallo Antiques, 222 East 83rd Street.

Sweet-Potato Cloverleaf Rolls (page 123): Nineteenth-century English Staffordshire transferware serving dish—Ages Past Antiques, 450 East 78th Street. English silver-plate pitcher, circa 1865—S. Wyler, Inc., 941 Lexington Avenue.

Kitchen Setting (page 125): All items in photograph are privately owned.

GARDEN PARTIES

Garden Opener

Table Setting (page 126): "Verdures" porcelain plates designed by Christian Tortu—Takashimaya, 693 Fifth Avenue. Stainless steel chargers by Mepra—Henri Bendel, Frank McIntosh Shop, 712 Fifth Avenue. "Phalsbourg" crystal wineglasses—Lalique, 680 Madison Avenue. Highball glasses—

Barneys New York, Madison Avenue at 61st Street. "Flemish" sterling flatware—Tiffany & Co., 727 Fifth Avenue. Organdy tablecloth and napkins with appliquéd embroidered leaves by Dransfield & Ross. For stores call (212) 741-7278. Pitcher—Crate & Barrel. For stores call (800) 323-5461. Potted herbs—L. Becker, 217 East 83rd Street. Steel café chairs with beechwood seats—Gardeners Eden, (800) 822-9600.

LUNCH IN THE COURTYARD

Tomato Bread Salad with Herbs (page 128): "Natural Ware" ceramic plate and "York" stainless-steel knife and fork by Calvin Klein Home. For stores call (800) 294-7978. "Evidence" crystal pitcher and "Brummel" crystal wineglass—Baccarat, 625 Madison Avenue. Cotton napkins by Anichini—Barneys New York, Madison Avenue at 61st Street.

SPRINGTIME ASIAN DINNER

Korean-Style Grilled Beef Short Ribs and Scallions (page 132): Ceramic plates and platter—Fishs Eddy, 889 Broadway. Cotton napkins—Pottery Barn. For stores call (800) 922-5507. Tin and wood table—ABC Carpet & Home, Inc., 888 Broadway.

Asian Cucumber Ribbon Salad (page 135): Bamboo chopsticks—Takashimaya, 693 Fifth Avenue.

Midori Lime Mousses (page 137): Hand-etched glasses; French acrylic flatware—Wolfman • Gold & Good Company, 117 Mercer Street.

COOL-OFF POOL PARTY

no credits

A FARMERS MARKET FEAST

Feta-Stuffed Eggplant Roll with Salsa Verde (page 142): "Star" ceramic service plates; ceramic salad plates; blue water glasses—Fishs Eddy, 889 Broadway. "Paris" stainless-steel flatware by David Mellor—Simon Pearce, 500 Park Avenue. Cotton napkins—ABC Carpet & Home, 888 Broadway.

Cod Fillet with Roasted Vegetable Ragout (page 144): Lyndt Stymeist ceramic dinner plate—Ad Hoc Softwares, 410 West Broadway.

REPAST IN THE SHADE

Table Setting (page 146): "The Bird" hand-thrown and hand-painted stoneware designed for Simon Pearce Pottery by Miranda Thomas; "Bell" hand-blown wineglasses and carafe—Simon Pearce Glass & Pottery, The Mill, Quechee, VT 05059. Italian cotton napkins—Frank McIntosh Shop at Henri Bendel, 712 Fifth Avenue.

Angel Food Cake with Cinnamon Plum Sauce (page 151): Mottahedeh "Cobalt Blossoms" majolica dessert plate for the Smithsonian Institution—Barneys New York, Seventh Avenue and 17th Street.

SUNDAY LUNCH ON THE VERANDA

Blueberry Tart (page 152): Nineteenth-century English ceramic dessert plates, linen napkins, decorated wood pantry box, homespun towel; bone and steel dessert forks, circa 1800—Gail Lettick's Pantry & Hearth, 121 East 35th Street.

Tomatoes (page 155): All items in photograph are privately owned.

Veranda Setting (page 156): Glass decanter—Casafina, Fields Lane, Brewster, NY 10509, (914) 277-5700. Hobnail glass—Pottery Barn. For stores call (800) 922-5507.

WATERSIDE ANTIPASTO BRUNCH

Melon with Prosciutto (page 158): Platinum luster porcelain dinner plate; "Cordova" sterling flatware by Elsa Peretti; "Optic" crystal wineglass—Tiffany & Co., 727 Fifth Avenue. Hand-painted linen napkins by Liz Wain (special order)—Gibraltar, 154 King Street, Charleston, SC 29401.

Table Setting (page 161): Holmegaard "Trigona" glass plate—Georg Jensen Silversmiths, 683 Madison Avenue. Gien "Ottoman" faience canapé plate—Baccarat, 625 Madison Avenue. "Ionic" stainless-steel flatware—Pottery Barn. For stores call (800) 922-5507. Glass bowl (olives); metal napkin ring—Frank McIntosh Shop at Henri Bendel, 712 Fifth Avenue. Glass beaker—Simon Pearce, 500 Park Avenue. Murano glass urn—Avventura, 463 Amsterdam Avenue. "Calliope" cotton fabric from the Benaki Collection—Brunschwig & Fils, 979 Third Avenue.

BIRTHDAY PARTY FOR THE KIDS

Pigs-in-Blankets; Baked Macaroni and Cheese; Coleslaw (page 164): "Moose Lake" china plates and mugs—Pipestone, 6 Onion Boulevard, Shrewsbury, PA 17361. Wooden boards—Williams-Sonoma. For stores call (800) 541-2233. Le Creuset enameled iron gratin dish—Bloomingdale's At Your Service, (212) 705-3170.

Cupcakes (page 168): All items in photograph are privately owned.

COCKTAILS AT FIVE

Curried Orange Pita Crisps; Orange and Apricot Rum Fizz (page 170): Linen cocktail napkin by Liz Wain—available at leading department stores.

Fresh Herb Pizzetta (page 173): Ceramic salad plate designed by Herman Fogelin for Grazia—Avventura, 463 Amsterdam Avenue.

SILVER ANNIVERSARY GARDEN PARTY

Champagne Punch (page 176): All items in photograph are privately owned.

Frozen Lemon Cream Meringue Cake (page 183): Faux mother-of-pearl silver-plate cake server—Wolfman • Gold & Good Company, 117 Mercer Street.

GETAWAY PARTIES

GETAWAYS OPENER

Picnic Setting (page 184): Blue glasses, cotton napkins, wood napkin rings, woven straw mats—Pottery Barn. For stores call (800) 922-5507. Wineglasses—Williams-Sonoma. For stores call (800) 541-2233.

AN APPLE ORCHARD PICNIC

Thyme-Scented Apple Galette (page 186): All items in photograph are privately owned.

Picnic Setting (page 189): Reversible denim and mattress ticking picnic cloth designed by Michael Formica for Chateau • X, (212) 477-3123.

A BEACH HOUSE LUNCH

Steamed Mussels with Orange, Fennel, and Garlic (page 190): Stoneware pie plate (mussels)—

Broadway Panhandler, 477 Broome Street. Yellow and blue Japanese ceramic bowls by Hakusan—Ad Hoc Softwares, 410 West Broadway. "Patrick" glasses—Crate & Barrel. For stores call (800) 323-5461. Linen towels—Bragard, 215 Park Avenue South, Suite 1801. Sutherland teak tray by John Hutton—Treillage, Ltd., 418 East 75th Street. "Hamaca Rojo" and "Hamaca Azul" fabric under tray (available through decorator)—Donghia Designs, 979 Third Avenue.

Porch Setting (page 192): "Pop" hand-painted wineglasses—Pottery Barn. For stores call (800) 922-5507. Glasses—Frank McIntosh Shop at Henri Bendel, 712 Fifth Avenue.

Swordfish Souvlaki (page 194): Lyndt Stymeist ceramic dinner plate—Ad Hoc Softwares, 410 West Broadway.

APRÈS-SKI SPICY FONDUE

Chipotle Cheese Fondue (page 196): French earthenware bowls (lids not shown)—Bridge Kitchenware Corp., 214 East 52nd Street. English pine table, circa 1890—ABC Carpet & Home, 888 Broadway.

Chocolate Wafer and Graham Cracker Brownie Cake (page 199): Cutting board—Dean & DeLuca, 560 Broadway.

LUNCH AFLOAT

Picnic Setting (page 200): "American Fitzhugh" enameled tin dinner plates by Robert Steffy—Kitchen Classics, Main Street, Bridgehampton, NY 11932. "Synergy" wineglasses by Block—for information call (212) 686-7440. Cotton beach towels—Ralph Lauren Home Collection, (212) 642-8700. "Stars and Stripes" hand-painted linen napkins by Liz Wain—Gibraltar Gallery, 154 King Street, Charleston, SC 29401, (803) 723-9394. "Primary Red Composition" cotton fabric (cloth), available through decorator—Schumacher, 939 Third Avenue, (800) 332-3384. "Picket" cotton chintz fabric by Waverly (cushions)—for information call (800) 423-5881. Rayon American flags—Old Glory Flag Company, 24 Pleasant Street, Cos Cob, CT 06807. Yacht courtesy of Witts End Charters, P. O. Box 625, Key Largo, FL, 33037, (305) 451-3354.

Grapefruit Rum Coolers; Curried Coconut Chips (page 202): Highball glasses—Pottery Barn. For stores call (800) 922-5507. Metal fish bowl. For stores call Mariposa (508) 281-2362.

Tailgate Party at the Game

Potato and Green Bean Salad with Citrus Miso Dressing (page 206): All items in photograph are privately owned.

Goat Cheese Polenta and Mushroom Tart (page 209): Cream "Crackle" dinner plate—Calvin Klein, 654 Madison Avenue.

A Day at the Beach

Getaways Picnic (page 212): Vintage wire basket with wooden handle (on back of bicycle); spatterware pail—Weeds, 14 Centre Street, Nantucket, MA 02554.

Lunch in the Meadow

no credits

Ice Skating Party

Doughnut Assortment (page 222): All items in photograph are privately owned.

Rich Hot Chocolate (page 224): French earthenware cup and saucer—E.A.T. Gifts, 1062 Madison Avenue.

CREDITS

The following photographers have generously given their permission to reprint the
photographs listed below; many have previously appeared in *Gourmet* magazine.

LANS CHRISTENSEN
"Nantucket in All Its December Splendor" (page 33).
Copyright © 1987.

JULIAN NIEMAN
"Half-Open Shutters in the Provençal Style" (page 149).
Copyright © 1994.

MATHIAS OPPERSDORFF
"Pumpkins in Strasburg, Pennsylvania" (page 45); "North
Light" (page 216). Copyright © 1989.

JOHN VAUGHAN
"Kitchen Setting" (page 70). Originally appeared in
Kitchens by Chris Casson Madden, copyright © 1993 by
Interior Visions Inc.

ROMULO YANES
"Tracing Garlic Through Eighteenth-Century Europe"
(page 118). Copyright © 1985.

Grateful acknowledgment is made to the following contributors
for permission to reprint recipes previously published in *Gourmet* magazine.

NAOMI BARRY AND BETTINA MCNULTY
"Chocolate Macaroons" (page 23); "Chocolate Custards"
(page 23). Copyright © 1992.

JOHN PHILLIP CARROLL
"Chocolate Doughnuts"(page 224); "Raised Doughnuts"
(page 225); "Maple Bars" (page 226). Copyright © 1991.

ROZANNE GOLD
"Lemon Rosemary Custard Cakes" (page 35); "Fresh
Herb Pizzetta" (page 173). Copyright © 1994.

MADHUR JAFFREY
"Broiled Coriander-Honey Chicken with Hot Sweet-and-
Sour Peanut Sauce" (page 39). Copyright © 1989.

LESLIE GLOVER PENDLETON
"Blueberry Tart" (page 157). Copyright © 1995.

MICHELLE SCICOLONE
"Almond Tart" (page 131). Copyright © 1992.

MICHELLE AND CHARLES SCICOLONE
"Chocolate Grappa Cake" (page 61); "Honey Grappa
Compote" (page 61). Copyright © 1991.

NINA SIMONDS
"Ginger Scallops with Stir-Fried Broccoli Rabe" (page
53). Copyright © 1994.

ZANNE EARLY STEWART
"Braised Pheasant with Red Cabbage and Wild Rice"
(page 14). Copyright © 1995. "Baked Brie en Croûte"
(page 66). Copyright © 1994.

Grateful acknowledgment is also made to Zanne Early Stewart for sharing her
cousin Martha Lordan's party planner with us for use in the design of our endsheets.

Claudette's birthday

Luncheon/Dinner   Date Sept.

Menu

Guests

Edith & B...
Jres and Ja...

breast of dove
...ing
...ells - watercress
rolls
...pepper - ...
...led mushrooms
...ch beans

Mr P

Jres   Steve of dove

...ances   Jane for

...ehe   F...

...ine 9

John

Luncheon/Dinner   Date Oct.

Menu   G

breast of wild dove   Annabelle & Fel...
telemeck tolls   Mall & Ra...
cavier theres   Jimmie ...

onion soup
pfeffernickle bread
chicken vermouth
mushrooms
cheese peas
endive salad + beetle
corn bread
English toffee ice-cream
cake for Jimmie's birthday

Wine Mint...
Dom R...

Flowers

swans - pink carnations

Gown & Jewels worn   ...seek satin P x - with sh...

Menu

...et of dove
...uched
...llops - mustard sauce   Mary L...
Lentle soup   Flor...
toast
chicken vermouth - mushrooms   Engl...
Cheese peas
endive + beetle salad